YOUR LIFE
IN YOUR HANDS

For Susan and Ruth

YOUR LIFE
IN YOUR HANDS
WRITING A PERSONAL JOURNAL

BRIAN HAWKER

Fount
An Imprint of HarperCollinsPublishers

First published in Great Britain
in 1991 by Fount Paperbacks

Fount Paperbacks is an imprint of
HarperCollinsReligious,
Part of the HarperCollins Publishing Group
77–85 Fulham Palace Road, London W6 8JB

Printed and bound in Great Britain by HarperCollins Manufacturing,
Glasgow

A catalogue record for this book is available
from the British Library.

CONTENTS

ACKNOWLEDGEMENTS

Keeping my personal journal has become a part of my life. I first became aware of the positive way of using a journal during a retreat experience some forty years ago. Since then I have attended Journal Workshops and am much indebted to the Ira Progoff School of Intensive Journalling in New York and many other friends who have encouraged me in exploring my life's journey by using this method of personal growth. Many of the ways in which I use my own journal and teach journalling to others owes much to their invaluable help and guidance.

I would like to thank all those who have allowed me to print extracts from their journals. To preserve anonymity all names have been changed. Each entry gives examples of what can be accomplished through the written word.

I should also like to thank my editor, Alan Mitchell, for all the help and encouragement he has given me in the writing of this book.

PREFACE

Journalling is about recording. If you can write a shopping list then you can keep a journal. It might be that I jot down in a scrappy notebook the names of the birds I have been watching; or I might describe the emotional response that my watching of a certain bird had on me — both the list and the effective writing are journal entries.

In this book I shall try to discuss the reasons for keeping a journal. I believe that the bare recording of facts, although interesting in themselves, is not enough. The journal I shall be describing and hopefully encouraging you to keep, will form an analysis of your life in order that you can answer three main questions:

1. Where have I come from?
2. Where am I now?
3. Where am I going?

When we enter the world we come without a manual of instructions. We are influenced by the whims and fancies of our parents, teachers, and those who hold authority over us. We make few major decisions of our own until we enter our late teens. In later life, our work and many of the things we engage in are directed by others. The journal we write will put us at the controls of our life. Hopefully, it will also allow us to keep away from the drudgery of an existence that we enter because we have not taken time to consider an alternative. To exist is not necessarily to live. To live we have to know where we are going and why. We have to become aware of our life purpose. We have to know where we have come from and how the past has affected the present moment. If we do not learn from our history we are doomed to repeat it — a tragedy we are all aware of in a century of two world wars.

Healing comes through an acknowledgement of past mistakes and this allows the freedom to let go those things which have hurt and dismayed us. It is only by letting go, not harbouring and thereby giving power to the injustices and hurtful remarks of others, that we have the will to live out our present moment.

Journalling allows us to get in touch with both our outer and inner worlds and although we cannot control either at times, we can at least gain an understanding that will enable us to live a more fruitful existence.

I hope that this book will lead you to review your life so that the past may be the past, the future be filled with hope and the present be an ever exciting and expectant moment.

1

INTRODUCTION TO JOURNALLING

Personal journal writing is not about recording history, making money from diaries or unearthing witty quips, although it will include all three. Writing a personal journal is an exercise in individual growth.

To record one's life is to become aware of the inner core self. It is to be able to hear and discern what that core self wishes to say and to be able to act upon it.

Each of us undergoes periods of spectacular growth. The changes that occur between childhood, adolescence and mature adulthood affect out relationship with others, with the world and our overall purpose in life. Life is always in movement if it is to be lived to the full. Without movement one is dead. Each year is a new year with new happenings and with new purposes to be fulfilled. If it isn't, then one is only recycling the previous year and there will be little or no growth in the existence of the individual. I am always saddened at farewell parties when the person retiring suddenly realizes that they haven't been teaching for twenty-five years, they have repeated twenty-four times what they taught in the first year. Or at silver wedding celebrations when it is realized that each of the past twenty-four years has only been a repeat of the first one, rather than a dynamic explosion of new experiences and awareness for each of those years.

To record the years would not only be of historical value but would allow the writer to review the dynamic of movement which has shaped the years. There is a need to experience ourselves as part of the momentum of life, rather than to be passive onlookers at an unstoppable turning globe.

To enter the reality of the movement there is a fundamental need to record what has happened. That is where the writing of a personal journal comes into its own. Daily, weekly, monthly or even perhaps only yearly, there is a need to take stock — to look at life objectively and to review the purpose and the principles which govern one's behaviour at the present moment.

Introspective writing is a contemplative way of asking the three main questions that will be discussed in this book:

1. What is happening for me at the now moment of my life?
2. What is my history?
3. How do I see my goals?

Journal writing that is mindful of these questions is certainly a positive way of ensuring that day-to-day living is not just a recycling of past mistakes and illnesses but an authentic attempt towards personal growth and wholeness.

One man who was sure of where he came from and where he was going was Stephen, the first martyr of the early Christian Church. Even when he was being stoned to death, he was able to 'see the heavens opened and the Son of man standing at the right hand of God' (Acts 7:56).

The journal should not be confused with a diary. The latter is used these days as a forward planning tool. In it is recorded the events and appointments for the coming days and months. The journal is a book in which one records the meaning and significance of the events and engagements; the relational attitudes and feelings towards individuals and the

2

emotions experienced during the course of the event. Let me give you an example of each:

> *Monday 7th September*
> 9 a.m. See Lawrence Smithy re new furniture for the office.
> 12 noon Lunch with Susan
> 3 p.m. Depart for conference at Blackpool.
> Ring Bill to tell him I shan't be at the committee meeting tonight.

That's an extract from a diary. It doesn't tell you much but it will control the day and therefore it has a very important purpose.

Later on the 7th September, the owner of the diary might begin to write his journal something like this:

> *Monday 7th September*
> The day started in a very morbid and depressing way. Clouds, wind, rain. This weather always makes me feel disheartened and this morning it was no different.
>
> Lawrence Smithy's proposals about office planning and the new furniture that would be required was equally disheartening. The thought that I shan't have my own office but just a space in an open plan area fills me with horror.
>
> Lunch with Susan cheered me up. She is very much into wedding plans and wanted me to approve the hall booking. She really is very lovely. I wish I was with her tonight. I think of her all the time and want to be with her. I imagine that we are married already. I am going to find it difficult to come away on conferences like this when we are married.
>
> I had a long talk with Bill when I phoned him about not being able to get to the committee meeting this evening. He was able to lift a lot of the depression I was still feeling or seemed to be building

up again. I wish I could get at the seat of what seems
to be the matter.
   Is it the office? Is it Susan? Is it the work load? Or,
and I suppose I have to face it, is it me?

The journal entry of the day gives greater insight into the
mind and feelings of the writer than does the diary entry. It
allows the writer to take stock of the day; to become
conscious of what is going on within himself and to
recognize the source of his strength. In this case he also
records his telephone conversation with Bill which makes
him ask questions about what is going on within himself.
Like us all he wants to project the depression on to others,
his work or even his fiancée, but comes to the conclusion
that he needs to look at himself.

   There are many people who have written journals like this
throughout the ages. *The Diary of an Edwardian Lady* is a
recounting of the days as seen through the eyes of a
particular person at a given time in history. It is interesting
for its everyday awareness of the beauty of the world in
which the writer lives.

   John Wesley, the founder of Methodism, kept a detailed
journal of his travels. He wrote his journal on a small leather
desk which was built on to the saddle placed on his horse.
It runs to some eight volumes in its published form. He
records his travels and the scriptures he preached about at his
various stopping places. It is to the journal that he unburdens
the inner movements of his soul and it is these reflections
that feed his prayer.

   The busy Swedish Secretary-General of the United
Nations, Dag Hammarskjöld, kept a book, not discovered
until 1961 after his tragic death in an aeroplane disaster, in
which he recorded his inner thoughts. *Markings* is a scattered
collection of meditations about the ways of a much-troubled

world and the inner effect of various events on one of the leading characters who tried to bring peace to this war-wearied planet.

Thomas Merton was a Cistercian monk in this century who did much of his writing in journal form. His *The Sign of Jonas* encouraged my own resolve to keep a journal. Like Wesley, Merton writes about both his inner search and what is happening in the outer world. From the silence of his Trappist monastery he is informed enough to reflect, write about and be involved in the outer events of his time which included the Vietnam War and the American involvement in it.

Not all published journals deal with the inner realities of life. A namesake of mine, although not a relative, James Hawker, published his *Journal of a Poacher*. In it he records the vicissitudes of his calling. It is both humorous and serious.

Perhaps the best known journal of all is *The Diary of Anne Frank*, the Jewish girl trapped in Amsterdam from 1942 until her arrest in 1944. As a journal it records the growing pains of an imprisoned adolescent. She recorded her thoughts and feelings which she could not share with another person in her cramped quarters. Anne Frank was killed in the concentration camp at Belsen. Her diary was first published in 1947 and has been the subject of a film and a television series.

Henri Nouwen, who gave up his successful career as a university professor in order to work with the mentally handicapped, records in journal form many of his meditations and thoughts which detail the awareness of his inner striving.

Historians often rely on journals. The evidence they contain, even if written from a subjecive viewpoint, gives historical perspective to a given period and place. Gerald of

Wales for example, in the twelfth century, penned a journal of his great tour of Wales which makes fascinating reading eight hundred years later.

Margery Kempe (a contemporary of Julian of Norwich and the other English mystics) wrote her *Booke* at the beginning of the fifteenth century and although not dictated by her until she was nearing the end of her life it records her thoughts and feelings as well as details of the people she met. Her journal 'Booke' provides a glimpse of the vicissitudes of a fourteenth-century housewife.

Politicians and their secretaries make money when they retire by publishing their diaries. Harold Macmillan's *Riding the Storm* and *Pointing the Way*, or John Colville's *The Fringes of Power – Downing Street Diaries 1939–1955* are good examples.

Jottings which when first scribbled down seem uninteresting, turn out to be gold nuggets when read at a later date. The epigrams of Oscar Wilde are a case in point.

Journals and diaries are the stuff of which politicians' memoirs are made. It is interesting to realize that after the heavy workload that many cabinet ministers carry, they sit down at night and record, albeit with an eye on publication, their feelings of the day's events. Tony Benn's *Out of the Wilderness, Diaries 1963–1967* and the subsequent volumes are an example.

Such journals have been of great historical interest but to write with an eye on publication does not always give the author a sense of absolute honesty. The type of journal writing we shall be discussing in this book requires an open, non-judgmental honesty. To be able to say, without fear of criticism, exactly what is happening in one's life is to enter into the true journalling spirit. To experience the feel and movement of life and to be able to record it objectively, laying it open to analysis, means that the writing will become a vehicle of personal growth and not just the recording of past events.

If you want to keep a record of historical events to pass on to your grandchildren or a local historical society, then do so. That is one way of keeping a journal. It is the way in which many of the journals I have already described were written.

However, the journal we shall be dealing with in this book is more than that sort of recording. It is a personal journal —personal in the sense of involving only oneself. It is a private thing — confidential, for your eyes only. It might even have a notice on it 'Please destroy without reading after my death.' Extracts from it could obviously be shared with a friend or a counsellor — someone whom you trust with your confidentiality.

Having decided to keep a journal, or at least to start one, the first thing is to determine what sort of book to use. This is a personal choice. Some people like to keep their writing in a special book, bound and perhaps even decorated. It is a way of honouring the contents and gifts of life. For others, of which I am one, a loose-leaf affair is easier. It is possible with such a system to keep like subjects together. Whatever sort of book you use there will be a need for an index. Do remember that with journal writing there are no rules. Find a book or a file, or the back of an envelope if that is the way you write, and get on with the story.

You might want to make entries in your journal throughout the day; that's fine. All you need to do is to enter the date (don't forget to add the year — it is surprising what tricks our minds play when we try to remember the year of an event!) and the time of the entry.

Most journal writers have special periods when they go to their writing. Some begin the day by writing down all the anxieties that have stayed with them overnight. Others write at the end of the day when they can reflectively consider what has happened during the past twenty-four hours. In the silence they try to feel the movement of their lives. While writing they objectively record that movement, not just of action but of feeling as well.

Keep your journal private. Tell your family, if they ask what you are doing, that you are recording your thoughts and feelings and tell them that what you are writing is confidential. If you have to, keep your journal under lock and key. You need a place where you can be honest with yourself; a place where you can write without fear of judgement and where censorship is unnecessary.

You will need pens and pencils, crayons and paints. Writing is not the only way of keeping a journal. I have seen a room full of clay models which record the ongoing life of a potter. Using representative pieces, the movement of life can really be observed. Use whatever materials you need. Some people will record by using mind-map outlines, others will want to write down the full experience, or use shorthand. Others still use symbols and small drawings or pictures. The choice is yours — after all, it is your life.

Some people cannot bear the thought of spending so much time in writing. That's OK. Use a tape recorder and dictate your thoughts and reflections. If you use this method, make sure you keep a record of where your entries are on the tape.

There is perhaps one warning. Journal writing is not for everyone. Carl Jung, the Swiss psychiatrist, wrote about the introverted and extroverted personality. The introvert gains energy from within the self, the extrovert relies on outside circumstances. The introvert likes to ruminate on things — doodle with possibilities. The extrovert likes to talk over possibilities with others. If you are an extrovert you will find the discipline of journal writing difficult, but not impossible.

If you are an introvert then don't get too bound up in just recording your life, make sure you live it. Don't over-write — use enough words to get down what needs to be set down and then leave it. You don't have to write a page when a sentence will do. Allow time for silence and reflection before, during and after the writing. Listen to the movement of your spirit.

Let's go to it.

With a sheet of paper in front of you, try to answer the question — Why do I want to keep a journal?

When you have meditatively written your answer to that question (remember there are no right or wrong answers) read the following examples of how others have tried to respond to it.

Diana, aged twenty-three
I used to keep a diary — I even had one of those five-year things. It had a little golden lock on it. I tried to make an entry in it every day. Now I want something more expansive. So many things are happening in my life and they keep getting jumbled up. I feel that I am missing something and I don't know what. I feel that if I keep a journal I shall be able to sort things out a little easier. I hope so anyway. The idea of a journal sounds grand — but it's not that I am looking for — more a sort of sounding board.

Alex, aged fifty
Why do I want to keep a journal? It raises questions as to whom I can tell my secrets to. When I was young I had my teddy bear, but now? Who really has time to listen to all my ramblings? And anyway, I find it difficult to trust people. I have realized of late that whenever I talk about me to someone else, I leave a bit of me with them and that can be painful. I've decided to write it all down without judgement

9

or censorship and see if I can make sense of it —
accept it and allow the daily happenings to guide me
in my life's pilgrimage. If the journal becomes an end
in itself, I shall stop keeping it.

Louise, aged seventy-one
I have kept a commonplace book for many years. I
cut out and put in it things that I have enjoyed.
Poems, pieces of good prose and so on. I have pieces
from the newspapers in it. I like to re-read some of
those papers — I have the papers of all the
coronations. Now I want to set down in some place
the sort of things my parents said to me when I was
younger. I want to recall my grandparents — they
lived such a different kind of life from mine. Perhaps
I will be able to pass on my journal to my children
or grandchildren. There is so much to say and at last
I have got time to write it all down.

Why not use your answer as a preface to your journal?

2

WHERE AM I NOW?

Life is more than a series of disasters which I have to understand before I am carried to my grave. The happenings in Coronation Street, Albert Square or Dallas are a microcosm of a nation rather than of one small segment of society. Television soap operas do not record the celebrations of life with the same intensity they use for the traumatic.

We all have periods of great rejoicing. Before looking at the harder realities of existence it is necessary to get in touch with the good and positive aspects. Out of the strength received from recalling the good events we can face the downhill slopes.

Have you ever considered the tremendous blessings you have received from life itself? Just list them in your journal now.

> I am thankful for my parents.
> I rejoice that I was able to have an education.
> I am thankful that I live in this place.
> I appreciate the freedom I have as an individual in society.
> I am grateful for my spiritual heritage.
> I rejoice in all the cultural activities that I enjoy – theatre, dance, opera.
> I am thankful for the sea, and the way it rejuvenates me when I am down.
> I consider it a blessing to be able to work.
> I am thankful for my husband/wife/partner and children.
> I am grateful for the food I eat and for all those who have had anything to do with its production.

I am thankful for my possessions and I think I am pleased that I don't feel too possessive of them. (I have a feeling that if I were too possessive my possessions would own me). I am thankful for time, and energy and health to do the things I want to do.

Beginning journal work by recording and honouring strengths rather than weaknesses, gives us a positive base from which to encounter the future.

A way of achieving this is through the practice of keeping a daily journal. In this section you will be able to record the events of the day. This, as I have already pointed out, will be more than just a diary entry. The account of the day will include the effect the day had on you. There is a need to record your feelings, the people involved and the context of the encounters as well as the effects of the event. Record the incidents that are taking place within the social sphere, any reading you are engaged in, things you have heard and the emotional responses they are having on you.

Remember that the events and their effects are not just either/or entries. They are both/and. One man wrote:

I feel as though I want to cry, or laugh. I am angry and yet I feel as though I am the happiest man alive.

If he could write, and thus take responsibility for his statements, the entry would have looked like this:

I am crying.
I am laughing.
I am angry.
I am happy.
All of these are happening within me at one and the same time.

12

The second entry gets at the ambiguity and expresses the true feelings. Owning to these feelings will allow him to deal with them, rather than pitting one against the other — asking questions like 'Am I happy or angry?' The truth is, he is both. The questions can then centre around the anger, the crying, the laughter and the happiness. 'What is it that I am angry about?' If I am angry, how come I feel so happy? What is the happiness trying to express? What are the tears saying to me? Are they tears of grief or happiness? How do I feel about my laughter? Is the event or experience really funny or am I just covering up my anxiety by laughing about it all?

Stop now. With a piece of paper in front of you, date it and then take time to record reflectively what has happened for you in the past twenty-four hours. When you have completed the exercise, read the following, which was written by Norman, aged thirty-seven, when he was facing a crisis in his life:

I am thankful for the time today to think out my present situation. I am thankful for the people around me who are supporting me at this moment. Particularly I am thankful for my wife Sheila and my children Mark and Elise and for my parents.

Job redundancy has made me feel redundant and there appears to be no immediate purpose for my life. Isn't it interesting that having written down a thanksgiving I can immediately see the flaw in that statement? I do have a purpose, even if it is only for those who are supporting me. *I am thankful for those who are supporting me.*

Security has always been a necessity in my life and when I got married I felt responsible for the security of Sheila. When the children came I felt the same responsibility for them. Now the parents are getting older and retired I feel responsible for them as well. Security has always meant an assurance that there would always be enough money to fulfil the immediate

needs. It is as though I am still following my parents'
message of never spending what I don't possess –
never getting into debt and so on.

Money is not an immediate need. I never thought
I would write a sentence like that but it is true. The
end-of-contract payment is enough to keep us for the
next six months. If that is true, and I think it is, then
what is really worrying me at this moment?

Purpose?

Security?

Money?

Or is it something else?

I think the latter. I feel humiliated for something
that is not and could never have been my
responsibility.

Yesterday all was going so swimmingly. I had a job
that I enjoyed. An income that adequately provided
for all our needs with some over for charity giving
and holidays. In the space of half an hour all that
seemed to change. Within those dreadful thirty
minutes I had been told by my immediate boss,
David, that the firm was closing and that my job was
redundant (I have to keep saying that *my job* was
redundant or else I think it is me that is redundant
and that is *not* true). I could have hit David I was so
angry. It was the timing, I suppose. 'Clear your desk,
report to personnel, collect your cheque and go.' All
like that. I could hardly believe it. In half an hour I
was on the street. I didn't return home immediately.
I wanted to work out what had happened. I was really
shocked and I suppose that I still am. When I got
home Sheila was as shocked as I. We talked and
talked about the situation and how I would soon get
another job and everything would be all right. I
didn't sleep a wink. I feel a failure (which is quite
stupid because I actually did a good job); I feel as
though the firm's closing is due to me (which is
ridiculous and gives me much more status than I
warrant).

When Brian suggested that I wrote it all down and

looked at it objectively I thought he was talking out of the top of his head. Somehow it all looks so different on paper and it appears manageable. I can even repeat one of his favourite phrases: 'Every problem is an opportunity.' I wonder.

Perhaps I do need to look at my lifestyle; perhaps I will look at the real 'needs' rather than the 'wants' of my life; this bombshell could be the start of something different which would give a deeper security and sense of purpose than I have ever had before.

I must add to my list of thanksgivings. I must add a thank you for the time out to really think what life is all about.

I know I am not going to sort this out in the next twenty-four hours – it might take weeks or even months. But if I can say right now 'That's OK', then at least I am into the acceptance of the situation as it is rather than bemoaning the fact that it has happened. At least it is a beginning. What about looking at the opportunities – opportunities for travel and. . . I must make a list.

It is strange how different a situation looks when it is committed to paper. By starting with his recognition of all that was good in his life, Norman was able to bring to consciousness the tremendous support that he had at this particular time. In his writing he was able to see that the things that had been talked about and thought about throughout the night (which were mainly concerned with money and security) were not the real issues that were troubling him. The loss of his job had given him time to reflect upon the purpose and meaning of life in a different way. Norman hasn't come to any conclusions yet but he has started. The problem has become an opportunity, the negative has turned to a positive purpose which is to seek out what he really feels is the meaning and rationale of his life.

Not all daily recordings will be as traumatic as this one. You may record the weather or what new plants have come into flower in your garden. If that is so, then try to record how you felt when you saw the first snowdrop or how you perceived the refreshing storm. Life encompasses a meaning that is deeper than our first thoughts about it. It is to be found in the understanding of the beauty of the first snowdrop — spring has come, life is bursting forth from the earth and I am a thrilling part of it.

To arrive at the depth meanings of some entries it helps to 'image' the moment. To do this, close your eyes, and let your mind centre around the particular event, or series of events. Allow images to present themselves to you. Try not to think of an image, let the picture present itself to you. Don't censor or judge the image, by saying, 'That's awful!' or 'Isn't that lovely!' Just watch the image and record what happens.

Norman, whose life had been shaken by his sudden unemployment, had the image of an old shoe. This is how he described it:

> I have this image of an old shoe. It has been thrown away and is now being worried by a puppy. The puppy picks up the shoe and bangs it several times on the road. After a while the puppy drops the shoe. Someone comes, picks up the shoe, puts it on and walks away.

In 'working' with this image, Norman was able to understand some of the inner dynamics in regard to his unemployment. He could see that the symbols of the shoe, the puppy and the 'someone' were all images of himself. He acknowledged that he felt as though he had been thrown away; that now he was being worried and banged about by all and sundry (specifically himself). He also recognized the hope evident in the image. The discarded shoe (himself) was eventually found and put to its proper use. Norman was particularly helped by the subsequent understanding that came from this image of himself. He enjoyed being worried by others and he likes working out his own problems even if they are painful at the time. That insight made him ask the question, 'What do I get out of being such a worrier?' He became aware that when he was having a hard time then other pressures such as mowing the lawn or painting the house receded. Sheila didn't put as much pressure on him at these times either!

In your daily journal include the events of the day — this needn't be just a rewrite of your personal diary engagements. Jot down the significant things that happened. If you are like me, it is possible to drive home on the motorway and down country lanes without being fully aware of passing certain exits or even seeing a bus-load of football supporters. Try, just for fun (as well as for good road sense), to be aware of the whole journey home. Leave the worries of the office or workshop behind. Talk to yourself — now I am aware of the red car trying to overtake me — I am aware of the flowers on the roadside... You will be surprised by the number of things that you had missed before you tried this awareness exercise. In your daily journal you might mention these new awarenesses. Soon you will find that you have left the worries of the office where they belong — at the office. There is something new for you to experience every single day. Don't miss it.

Writing your daily entry need not take up a lot of your time. Ten or fifteen minutes at the end of the day helps to relax you and allows you to let go of the frustrations — the 'pay off' is that you won't have to worry before going to sleep.

3

TO SLEEP,
PERCHANCE TO DREAM

The daily journal entry would be incomplete without some reference to dreams. Dreams are the nightly visitors who speak to us in their own symbolic form. Their way of communication can be warming, frightening, calculating or depressing. As dreamers we need to listen to them, for they often complement our waking moments.

Our place in the universe is to be responsible co-creators with the architect. In order to fulfil this function we need to be in contact with the creator. Through dreams such contact is possible.

The earliest recorded dreams can be found in the Bible. Jacob's dream at Bethel (Genesis 28:10–22) of the ladder set up between earth and heaven, gave him a sense of the presence of the divine in his life and a reassurance about his life journey. From the dream encounter came the contract that Jacob felt able to make with the creator.
In brief:

1. Jacob dreamed.
2. Jacob interpreted the dream.
3. Jacob acted on the dream.

It would appear that one of the ways by which the divine gets in touch with the created is through dreams. Through symbolic imagery, because we seem unable at times to listen to or interpret the signs of the day, we are forced to listen to the messengers of the night.

All dreams follow Jacob's pattern:

1. I dream and record the dream.
2. I come to some way of interpreting the dream.
3. I act on the dream.

Some dreams are prophetic. They may well be asking us to take some action that will affect our future. I think that such dreams are rare but they do occur. They come at times of important change when we are resistant to all other forms of communication. Like all dreams they need to be authenticated by others before we act upon them.

Other dreams place into perspective the happenings of the day; they give us a new understanding of a particular action that has already taken place. Norman, whose job was made redundant, dreamed two or three nights later about himself and his family falling off a high cliff. The dream authenticated the work of the previous days when all looked so bleak, as though they were in fact falling off a cliff, coming to an end of that particular period of their lives.

Dreams may also be the way in which we are told some truth about ourselves which helps the inner journey to proceed. Often such dreams are a sort of allegory where the symbolism speaks in a way that is meaningful to us.

If we believe that dreams are important then we must record them as soon as we wake up. Use your journal for this. Make sure that you have a piece of paper and a pen or pencil by your bed. Dreams, unless recorded on first waking, will disappear. If this happens and the dream is an important one it will be repeated.

Once your dream has been recorded you need to understand it and begin to come to some tentative interpretation of it.

It might help you to try the following exercises in your journal.

Your Life in Your Hands

1. Record a dream. Try to write the dream in the first person present tense as though the dream were happening at this moment. 'I am sleeping in a bed that is floating on a cloud. I see people floating around me. A woman, whom I do not know, comes forward and gives me a plate of toast...'
2. Give the dream a title. This will help you to locate the dream at a later date. Such a title could well be connected with the content of the dream. Jacob's dream at Bethel could be called 'The Ladder'.
3. Try to see what the theme of the dream is. The theme of Jacob's ladder dream is 'the communication between earth and heaven and the nearness of God to me'.
4. As gently as possible try to write down the effect the dream had on you. What are your thoughts and feelings about it? Jacob (Genesis 28:16) felt afraid; he felt that God was in this place; he understood his own lack of knowledge and awareness of the presence of God; he became aware that wherever he is, that place is the gate of heaven.
5. What question is the dream asking you? In the case of Jacob the dream was asking if he thought himself self-sufficient.
6. Ask yourself what action you need to take as a result of your dream. Jacob needed to build an altar. He needed to make a contract with God (Genesis 28:20–22).

In brief when you have a dream:

1. Record the dream as though it were still happening.
2. Give it a title.
3. What is the theme of the dream?
4. What is your emotional response to the dream?

5. What questions is the dream asking you?
6. What action needs to be taken to honour the dream?

You might find the symbolic language used in the dream difficult to interpret. Such language is used because we have failed to understand the signs we have been given when we are consciously awake.

In your own dreams each symbol may well need to be looked at separately and teased out for its meaning. If this is done reflectively, then the meaning that is appropriate for you will become apparent. Let me give you an example:

In the dream, 'I am sitting in a small room. The walls are covered with various patterns that seem to tell a story. I am aware that although I feel alone there is something else in the room...'

The dream goes on, but for the purpose of the example I want to take the symbol of the 'small room'.

In the centre of a piece of paper put the words 'small room'. Then write down your associations with it.

Mother's workroom

attic box room...   :   ...claustrophobia

SMALL ROOM

the loo...   :   ...cupboard under
the stairs

My study

Do this for each of the symbols represented in the dream. In the example we would have to look at the symbol of the patterned wall stories.

Something with a beginning
and an end

Beano... : ...cartoon strip

PATTERNED WALL STORIES

ceiling frieze... : ...Bayeux Tapestry

Nursery rhyme wallpaper

Make sure as you do this that you always return to the symbol. Don't make chains or word associations (e.g. 'small room'... mother's workroom, ironing, sewing, recipe planning, etc.).

Carl Jung suggested that when you have completed such a review of the symbols an 'Aha' moment of realization would occur. In some psychologically unexplained way the true interpretation of the symbol becomes apparent. The putting together of the series of 'Aha' moments will give you a tentative interpretation of the dream.

Before you act on a dream check it out carefully with a friend or counsellor. Ask yourself the following questions:

1. Is this dream about some aspect of my life that I am hiding?
2. Is there something in this dream which I need to face?
3. Is there something in this dream which concerns another person? What is it?

4. Does this dream have a message that I need to receive and act upon?
5. What needs to be done?
6. How am I going to do it?
7. With whom can I share this dream?

Not all dreams are easy to interpret. Some defy interpretation for many years. Others have to be worked at over a long period of time before their truths become apparent and any action regarding the dream can be taken.

The journal allows you to record the dream so that you have it for study. You may start to work with it — giving it a title, a theme, and recording your emotional response to it quite quickly — but the interpretation becomes stuck. Don't worry about this. Leave it for a while and come back to the entry in your journal at intervals. Some people work on their dreams over a period of years. This would be especially true of the so called 'big dream' — the life-changing dream. Other dreams may well give you clues to understanding and interpretation.

Sometimes you will have a dream series when one aspect of a dream recurs. You might dream in serial form when one dream follows another. Your journal collection of dreams may well give you insight into linking messages which are of significance to you. Insights may affect your life and your course of action. Carl Jung believed in his dreams and was not afraid to honour them by some action. It takes courage to do that.

Try not to use dream symbol dictionaries. Each symbol is unique to you and only you. There are some archetype symbols but these also have to be found by you, interpreted by you and brought into your situation. An archetype symbol is one that is common to many and thus comes from the collective unconscious* as opposed to the symbol that comes from the personal unconscious. The earth-mother is one such archetype symbol, but its meaning becomes personal to the dreamer and carries with it the wisdom of the collective unconscious.

Here are some exercises to help you get into the exciting world of a dream work.

1. Record a dream. Use the first person present tense as though the dream were happening now. Don't be afraid of how silly it sounds or looks when you have written it down. Dreams use symbolic language to convey their meaning and the more ridiculous they sound and look on paper the more likely the message will be received.

When you have written your dream you might like to read the following dream which was recorded by Len, a fifty-six-year-old counsellor.

> I am walking into a state room. The room is Palladian in style. Chandeliers are hanging from the ceiling and giving a soft light to the whole proceedings. A lot of people are coming and going with flunkeys serving cocktail food. I am dressed very informally in jeans and a tee-shirt. The others are all formally dressed. The Prince and Princess of Wales enter the room and begin to greet guests. A person comes to me and says that I will have to do something about them as their marriage is in a muddle. Charles comes to me and says that one must look for inner meaning to life. When Diana comes to me she says that one must get on with life and not just navel gaze. I don't reply. I keep my own counsel.

* The collective unconscious contains material that is common to many people and races. The personal unconscious contains material that appertains only to the individual.

Once you have recorded the dream you are ready to work with it.

2. Give your dream a title.

In our example the title is 'Royal Counsellor'. The title reflects the main elements of the dream and will be an easy one to recall should the dream be repeated or enlarged at a later date. The title helps us to find the dream easily in our records.

3. State briefly the theme of your dream.

> E.g. Counselling in high places with the rich and wealthy, with whom I am not comfortable (witness my inappropriate clothes; the jeans and tee-shirt). The dream also brings to awareness the difference between inner and outer counselling (witness the different statements made by Charles and Diana).

4. State the effect your dream had on you.

> E.g. The dream had the effect of bringing me to a realization of the grandeur of the job I do – helping others. It also made me feel very humble. (I am among the great.)

5. What questions does your dream ask you?

> E.g. As a professional counsellor the dream was asking me all sorts of questions. Do I only counsel the rich because they are the ones who can afford to pay? What is the extent of my help to the less fortunate who cannot afford to pay? How do I deal with the inner and outer directions of my own life?

N.B. The questions refer to you, the dreamer. Don't get caught up in letting the dream ask you questions about the state of Charles and Diana's marriage. They are just symbols in the dream to help you look at what is happening for you.

6. What action do you need to take to honour the dream?

> E.g. I need to give a percentage of my time to the less fortunate who need counselling but who perhaps cannot afford to pay.

N.B. In order to honour the reality of the dream the proposed action needs to be something that can be put into effect within the next week.

This immediate dream interpretation may be all that is necessary for the particular dream you have chosen. It may be all that is required for many of your dreams. Its advantage is that it is quick and easy to do. For some dreams the interpretation is not so obvious and there is a lot of deeper work to be done. Or you might find that the dream you had given an immediate interpretation to comes up in a different form the following night or even the following week, month or year. In that case there is something deeper to look at and you will have to analyse the dream symbol by symbol.

The counsellor who had the dream we worked with a little while ago had such an experience. It took him back to look at the dream and his immediate interpretation. In turn he looked at the various symbols:

A Palladian-style state room
Chandeliers
Soft light
Lots of people
Flunkeys
Cocktail food
Informal clothes
Formal clothes
The Prince of Wales
The Princess of Wales
Request
Marriage meaning
Inner Meaning

Getting on with life
Navel gazing
Keeping one's own counsel

Some interesting things were revealed as he looked at the symbols. He realized that the 'Aha moment' with chandeliers and soft light had something to do with not seeing the whole thing in its true light. This seemed to be confirmed by the flunkeys (i.e. people dressed to be other than they really are) who served cocktail food (something that is not filling). He also came to an awareness that people in formal clothes presented an image they wanted you to accept, whereas his own informal clothes in the dream represented a much more laid back approach to truth. The arrival of the Prince and Princes of Wales reminded him in the 'Aha moment' that the Prince of Wales is only an heir, he is not yet the King, he is in waiting for the great event to happen and this can only come about through the death of the Queen. The dreamer asked himself what great event he was waiting for and what he was doing with his time before that event happened. Who or what had to die within himself before the prince in him could take his rightful place? The request to do something about the marriage made him look at his own difficulties in marriage and the muddle he seemed to be experiencing. He realized that he kept his own counsel about his own marriage frustrations and felt this was just navel-gazing. He was alerted to the importance of the inner life (as an introverted personality this was attractive to him). He was warned that he needed to get on with the outer events of life, to participate rather than withdraw into his own thoughts.

The immediate interpretation was not invalidated by this further work but was enhanced by it. It showed how the dream can be looked at on several different levels. All levels had some aspect of the truth which could reinforce his life and the way he operated. He knew he was looking at the presenting problems of his own marriage and the frustrations caused by it. There were other things to work on besides the action which was to help the less fortunate (something he had understood from his immediate interpretation). In this case he was the less fortunate and he interpreted afresh his own jeans and tee-shirt in the Palladian state room to remind him of his own needs.

Len wanted to honour the dream by some action. This action included his first interpretation to help the less fortunate to receive counselling. Now one in ten of his clients are given a free consultation. When he looked at the second interpretation he realized that he had to do something about his own marriage – he sought a counsellor from Relate and worked on the things that were bothering him. He and his wife had several interviews before coming to a conclusion about their marriage. He also knew that there were things within him that needed pursuing – his inner life journey was calling him to make changes in many of the things that he was doing. He also became aware that this interest with the inner journey was taking time from the things which he ought to be doing in the outer world. He sought aid from his grandfather, whom he had always considered to be a wisdom figure for himself. He could have had a journal dialogue with a wisdom figure (see p.31).

Look again at your own dream and the interpretation. Do you need to take it further? If so, how? Try an analysis of the dream symbols in more detail than the immediate reflection and write the results in your journal.

Don't be overwhelmed by the new things you learn about yourself when doing an exercise such as dream interpretation, nor let yourself become depressed by what the dream seems to reveal. You have lived with yourself for a long period of time. Perhaps you are stuck, life appears to have landed you in a rut. The dream and its explanation enables you to move. To change your principles. To check on your assumptions. To look for new pathways, new ways of doing things. To enter realistically into the movement of your life and not just to be a passive spectator of a seemingly static situation.

I have already spoken of Carl Jung's awareness of the existence of archetypes or the symbols which are part of the dream world but also a part of the collective unconscious. Often these dream symbols correspond to images that appeared in ancient myths, art and religion. The dreamer would not have known about these myths in his or her conscious state. They come from another place and another time. Archetypes are types of personality that recur over and over again.

There is an immense list of archetypes but they all fall into a basic pattern. One pattern has to do with 'making a journey' – so you get the pilgrim, the wanderer, the hermit and Christian of *Pilgrim's Progress*, who are all archetypes. Or 'the hero/heroine' – King Arthur, Parsifal. Or another main archetype line is that of 'the adversary' – the devil in all sorts of guises, the enemy, your own shadow side (the part of you that you don't look at, the hating, murderous side of yourself). Yet another main line of archetype deals with 'death and rebirth'. The ancient myths are full of examples of the gods dying and being reborn. In a symbolic language this often comes about through dreaming about a murder but you know that the person is not dead. They have passed through an experience of rebirth. The other main archetype line deals with what Jung called 'The *anima* or *animus*' – the male or female side of our personality (*anima*, the feminine side of the man; *animus*, the masculine side of the woman).

Our unconscious and conscious understanding of Jesus Christ is part of our understanding of archetypes. He holds within himself the archetype of the heroic pilgrim on a journey who faces the adversary devil and has to come to terms with his own death and rebirth. By moving away from the pervading attitude of the Jewish confrontational maleness he shows the softer, feminine caring side of himself that does not compromise his essential masculinity.

We also are a mixture of the archetypes. In our dreams the same will be true and the symbol presented may well be a 'wise person who is on a journey' — the pilgrim; or a 'murderer out to get us in his speeding car' — the adversary, shadow of ourself; or perhaps you are aware that in the dream 'you are about to die' — death/rebirth. The dream doesn't mean that you are about to die physically but that within you there is a need to allow a particular desire, assumption, belief or work, to die in order that a new thought or action can live.

The question that comes in dream interpretation is, 'What do I do with an archetype symbol when I come up against it in a dream?'

One of the ways of answering that question is to dialogue with the archetype in the dream. Perhaps the figure is that of a wise woman — what is it that she wishes to say to me? In dialogue form it is possible to ask that question and to receive a reply which can come from the unconscious part of yourself. This reply may well need clarification and in the dialogue process it is possible to tease this out. In this exercise we give the archetype symbol a voice and through the silence we hear and record what that voice says.

Let me give you an example from a dialogue written and meditated upon by Jane, a lady aged seventy-one.

Before starting to dialogue make sure everything is ready — your pens and pencils, paper, handkerchief. Then sit quietly and begin to relax yourself. Let all the tensions be eased from the body. Close your eyes and recall the dream figure.

In her dream Jane had been visited by a 'mother-earth figure' whom she felt had a message and a certain wisdom to impart to her.

In the dialogue the lower case figures represent the dreamer, the capital letters represent the archetype mother-earth figure's response.

I am sitting quietly in my chair. I am thinking about the mother-earth character that appeared in my dream. In the quietness I re-enter the dream. I become aware of the presence of mother-earth. She is dressed in a long green dress made of hessian. Her features are brown and seem to have been carved by the wind. Her hair is grey and long. She has a smile that invites one in. I am not afraid but seem to be searching for the right question and yet I know that I don't have to find it. There is a 'knowing' without knowing. Things are all right. I look at mother-earth and say very gently, 'I am here to listen to what you have to say to me.' At first there is no reply. I seem to be listening to a silence that is thundering. After what seems to be a very long time there is a response. LISTEN TO THE SILENCE. HEAR THE BREATHING OF THE TREES AND THE SYMPHONY OF THE WIND. RAISE YOUR EYES AND LOOK ABOUT YOU. BECOME AWARE OF THE DESTRUCTION YOU HAVE CAUSED AND LEARN FROM IT. I felt devastated. Everything was my fault. There was a long silence. Then, very meekly I asked, 'How? How can I learn from the muddle and the destruction you say I have caused?' I waited for a reply. I was still conscious of her presence, as real as she had been in the dream which had dealt with the break-up of my marriage, the financial collapse of my ex-husband's business and the disastrous results it had on my son and daughter. Out of the silence came a response.

LISTEN TO THE SILENCE.
As I waited I became conscious of tears running down my cheeks as the events of the past forty years re-enacted themselves before me. I saw my ex-husband and the awful publicity that greeted the collapse of the business. I saw us moving house and the effects it had on the children. I went through the

agony of the divorce and my own new marriage. I
was aware of a new sort of understanding.

LISTEN TO THE SILENCE. HEAR THE WORDS OF THE SEA
AND THE SKY. THE SEA ROARS AND THE SKY CRIES BUT
EACH IN TIME BECOMES CALM AND AT ONE WITH THE REST
OF THE CREATED ORDER.

'How do I become one with the mess?'

THE EBB AND FLOW OF THE TIDE CANNOT BE STOPPED,
NOR THE RAIN RETURNED TO THE CLOUDS, BUT THE
EARTH WILL BE WATERED AND PRODUCE AGAIN AND THE
SEA PROVIDE LIFE FOR THE FISH.

My tears were stilled. I sat back and considered
mother-earth's words. I don't think I fully
understood them and writing them down seemed to
be a help. They seemed to be saying that I could not
stop what had happened but I could do something
about the rest of my life. My life still had a
productive part and there was room to swim. I was
greatly heartened by the conversation. It gave me a
sense of direction and yet to the outsider it would
have meant little. I share it because I am aware that
I have started living my life again, the storms are
accepted but they are over; there is a new marriage,
I have made contact with the children again. The
storm has changed the lie of the land but it is still
land and it is still productive.

Through dialogue this woman has become aware of the ongoing dynamic of her life. She has come to terms with the
storms which had threatened to overwhelm her she can look
ahead to a rich future.

You will notice that the dialogue is produced from a
patient waiting in the silence. Even mother-earth asks the
woman to 'listen to the silence', to the inner working of
acceptance and movement. Many dialogues come from the
silence. Journal writing is not just about penmanship!

If dialoguing doesn't help, why not try writing a letter to
the person concerned. In Len's dream, he decided to write

a letter to the Prince. He was able to say something about the reception, how he had felt out of place and incorrectly dressed. He has teased out the dream interpretation from a different perspective.

> Dear Prince,
> I am writing to you because I wish to explain my behaviour at the recent reception. I felt out of place and certainly incorrectly dressed for the occasion.
> I apologize for not treating you with the respect that you deserve.
> Although I am writing to you, the Prince, I recognize within myself that you are a part of me; the part I have never respected and always tried to avoid. Hence my distaste for receptions of this nature. Somehow you are a representative for me of the whole established order of life that I have always tried to evade.
> I recognize in the correctness of things at the reception that law and order do have a part to play in my life and that I cannot continue trying to avoid responsibilities by acting so fatuously. My dress was a way of expressing my contempt for what was an important moment in my life.
> In apologizing for my tardiness I intend to look again at the way I treat the Prince within myself and my behaviour towards others.
> > Yours because mine,
> > Len

Of course the letters don't have to be sent — they would in any case be meaningless to the recipient. The purpose of writing the unsent letter is to help in the understanding of the dream. Dreams can be interpreted only by the dreamer. Others can help you clarify the dream, but only you know the correct interpretation.

Together with your daily journal, this dream journal should prove an invaluable aid to your own life-analysis.

4

WHERE HAVE I
COME FROM?

We all have a history. I am not alone in this world and have never been so. We come from our parents and we are related to others. We live in an interdependent world. We are all a part of the pattern we call life. Rather like a jig-saw puzzle, we only see the pieces we are placing into position at the present moment. We have some idea of what the finished jig-saw will look like but its exact colours and hues are not available all the time.

To get in touch with the patterned jig-saw of our lives we need to fill in the background. Our history is important. From it we learn how to relate to other members of our family, to society and to the world. If we are not aware of our history and the lessons we have learnt from it then we shall repeat it again and again until the message has been assimilated. The repetition is a recycling, it is very costly time-wise and can be extremely painful.

A battered wife who divorces one husband and then marries another who treats her in the same way is repeating a pattern. Until the prime lesson is learnt (perhaps she was constantly disciplined by her father and this was the only way she could gain his attention) she will go on recycling her life. The pain and distress are enormous and necessary until the lesson is learnt that there are other ways of being loved.

The journal exercise to arrive at some of our background history is to construct a ladder where each step is a significant movement in life. Like a ladder the step can be very short, but it leads to the next one. Like ladders the way of construction can be very different – long ladders, short ladders, step ladders, roof ladders and so on.

In the journal exercise my life history can be looked at from different angles. Thus I could construct my ladder steps from the point of view of straight history like this:

1. I was conceived.
2. I was born.
3. I went to school.
4. We moved house.
5. I had my first girl friend.
6. Started work.
7. Got married.
8. Had children.
9. Became a widower.
10. Found new interests.

The ladder could be constructed by listing the houses or counties I had lived in. Or you might want to be more explicit about each step:

1. I was a twinkle in my father's eye.
2. Born 1949 in California. The second child.
3. We moved to England where my father was attached to the American embassy in London.
4. Play school followed by infant school in England – my mother insistent that I join the English system. My father not happy about this.
5. Junior school. Made lots of friends who thought I was very rich because I was an American.
6. My first visit to America to see my American grandparents and cousins. It was very strange and I felt out of place.
7. When we returned to England we moved to a house in Hertfordshire and my father travelled to London daily.
8. The local grammar school. I did well and enjoyed it. Lots of friends of both sexes. I started to menstruate and went through a funny stage which was fairly unhappy. I felt fat.

9. The second visit to America. Felt more like an English woman than an American one, although we all had a lot of fun. My grandparents seem very old.
10. University and my first really big love affair. Got badly hurt and went off boys for a long time.
11. Met Kevin and after graduation, got married. I guess I'm English now.

Exercise: Construct your own ladder. If possible put in dates.

As you thought about that exercise many other ways of constructing it will have come to you. How about a ladder of all the eventful things that have happened in the world since you were born? To construct a national or international ladder of your own years would really put you in the context of history.

You may well see patterns even when writing the ladder, that will help you to look carefully at the movement of your life.

Once the ladder has been completed, each step becomes the heading of a chapter of your own book of life. Each step needs to be written up in some detail, bringing into the entry the people, places and events as well as the remembered feelings of the period.

Exercise: Choose one of the steps on your ladder and wrote it up.

When you have completed the exercise you might like to read the following journal entry of Lesley, who write the second of our ladder illustrations.

I was four when we moved to England in 1953.

My mother had married my father during the war and returned to the US with him after the declaration of peace in Europe in 1945. She had lived in a small village in Dorset and we consequently had grandparents here when we arrived. There was Mother and Father, my brother George, who had been born in 1947, and me (born 1949). So George was six and I was four.

I want to write about this period of my life now because somehow it affected me in various ways throughout my life and I wonder if it still has some energy going for it.

In America I felt American. When we arrived in England it was so different. Mother hadn't been back since 1945. She loved America and everything American. She got on well with Granpy and Gramma (Father's parents) and with all the cousins and aunts and uncles.

Granpy was my special favourite and I guess I was his. I was the only girl grandchild and consequently I think he spoiled me a lot.

When we got to England and went to Dorset before we found our London flat it was all so strange. Mother was unhappy and Father didn't know what to do. He seemed so out of place. Everything was so small and we were all on top of one another. My new grandparents seemed to live a very sheltered life in the village and the Women's Institute was more important to Grandmother than anything else.

On that first visit we only stayed for a week before the flat in London was ready for us. My father was going to work in the American Embassy and wanted to get on with things. The grandparents were very worried about us going to the 'big city' as they called it. It was as if the whole place was immoral and likely to be blown to smithereens by the devil. Grandmother kept saying to Mother, 'You will be careful, won't you?' and 'Don't go out on your own. All those Teddy boys about. It is very dangerous.' Looking back on it now, it is funny — I didn't even know what a Teddy boy was and I thought that the creature must be a cross between my brother George and my teddy bear. When I saw my first real live Teddy boy I couldn't take my eyes off of him. His long hair and beautiful clothes which were so colourful was great.

London was a small girl's dream. George and I were taken everywhere. Buckingham Palace and Westminster Abbey where the Queen had been crowned. There was an air of excitement in the city.

Father was very busy but we went to the Embassy at times and had lots of children's parties. It was all fun except for Dorset and Grandmother and Grandfather. I came to know them better over the years but at that time they were strangers and I vowed that if I had grandchildren I would certainly make sure I saw them and got to know them better before they were six and four. Writing this now I can see how difficult it must have been for them as well. I hadn't realized that they had never ever been to London, let alone lived in the city. They rarely travelled in those days. They treated my mother as though she still wore gym slips and had funny teeth. I suppose they were protective and possessive. They had lost their daughter to America as a result of the war and they didn't want to lose her and the family to the city where they could escape again from the maternal clutches.

As I look back now I am very aware that there was always tension whenever we went to see them. In the early days I don't think they ever came to see us. I am also aware that Mother was a different person when she was with them, when she thought she would be with them, and when she had been with them. There was an anxiety fear which seemed to communicate itself to us all. We were scrubbed and always dressed in our best. We were shown off in the village, and being little Americans we roused a certain amount of jealousy and hostility. Again I didn't realize this until a lot later. Many of the unmarried men in the village felt that the American GI's had stolen their women while they were away at war. We also had a higher standard of living than anyone we ever came across in the village.

As I have been writing this I have become very aware of my own anxiety fear and love of justice which I suppose could well have come from this period of my life. I am also aware that I still treat elderly people with kid gloves as though I am afraid of them. This never happens when I am in the States (there are different problems when I am there because as a result of my upbringing here in England I don't belong there

38

either). Somehow if we had been received with the open warmth of America when we had come I feel I would have grown up quite different from my anxious self today.

There are a lot of things going on in that extract. They deal with people, especially the English grandparents and the important discovery of the mother/daughter relationship between the generations. There is also mention of jealousy and hostility. Lesley is also aware of the likelihood of these events being trigger areas of her own anxiety and fears. By writing her history she is beginning to understand and hopefully come to terms with her past. In learning about her past she will be strengthened for her future.

In journalling it is not uncommon for the writer to have an insight into a past event which still has bearing upon the present behavioural pattern. The recycling event is prevented in this extract by the emphatic statement that when the writer has grandchildren she will get to know them early on in their lives. The statement has been made about a future event while reliving and writing about an historical actuality.

Always re-read your journal entries. Underline statements that repeat patterns. Often they are not noticed for their importance at the time of writing.

The other point to mention while dealing with this extract is that Lesley takes responsibility for her own behaviour and her own anxiety fears. She recognized where they came from, her mother and her grandmother, but she does not blame them for her own state. To blame them for her present unhappiness with the way she is living is to say that nothing can be done about the situation. That is untrue. Taking responsibility for the problem opens the possibility for change within the self. But leaving it as a projection – 'I am like this because my mother was afraid of my grandmother' – will preserve the status quo.

Lesley worked with her ladder step by writing a dialogue with her mother and grandmother. She also used the 'unsent letter' exercise by writing to her American grandparents. In her daily journal for the day she wrote:

> I have just finished writing an unsent letter to my Granpy and Gramma. I have been able to tell them all that they meant to me in the early years of my life. Strangely, as I was writing it I started to cry. I hadn't thought about them for a long time. I released a lot of pent up grief. I wonder how my father dealt with all this? Perhaps I need to ask him. I owe a lot to my parents and grandparents on both sides of the Atlantic. The meekness and retiring nature of my mother's parents and the extroverted fun of my Granpy and Gramma were in stark contrast to one another. But I am a product of their genes. I am half British and half American. It has caused difficulties but after writing my dialogues and unsent letter I at last feel that I understand it all. I needn't be afraid of the past, nor do I need to duplicate it.

In order to obtain a full history each of the ladder steps need to be written up in full in the same way. When you have finished writing up the ladder then construct another ladder from a different point of view — write that up in the same way. Continue doing this until you have a complete analysis of your life from every conceivable angle. It will take a long time but if it stops you having to repeat your own or your family's mistakes then the time it costs is but a small price to pay for the freedom of an exciting future.

As you write you will become conscious of certain patterns in your life. You may become aware that every time you meet a new person you retreat into a shell, become tongue-tied, or that you flirt with people of the opposite sex but never make a commitment to anyone. You may realize that you always make decisions in the same way; either too quickly or by procrastination. Whatever it is that comes to light as a pattern can be dealt with. The greatest hurdle is always in the recognition. Once I know that I am a procrastinator I can ensure a behavioural change that will stop that tendency without going to the opposite extreme of making a change too quickly and without enough facts. By writing about the projected change in my journal I honour the work I have done in the review of my life.

Another aspect of my life history is that of my health record. Bodily health affects the way I lead my life. If I am constantly having headaches or backaches then I respond to situations and people in a different way than if I am free from such pain. If I constantly take drugs (prescribed or not) then my actions will be affected and my feelings will not necessarily be reliable pointers to my real state of being. If I have a fit and well-disciplined body then my insights and intuitions will be heightened.

We receive many blessings through our bodies that are not available to all people. Our sight is an example. I am aware of the beautiful colours of autumn, of the glory of a rainbow or the blaze of the sky at sunset. The gift of sight is one of the aspects of life denied to a blind person. I give thanks for my sight.

Touch is another blessing. The feel of someone's hand on my shoulder when I cry or the loving embrace of a child are all part of the joys that I receive through my body.

The same is true of my taste buds, of the things I hear and smell. When any of the five senses are not working then I am a deprived person.

My body is the vehicle in which I live my life. It does not come with an instruction book and yet it is the most precious possession I shall ever own. Unless I cherish it and regularly service it my body will let me down. These occasional lapses or illnesses are signs which speak to me and I would be foolish if I did not listen to what they are saying.

Your Life in Your Hands

One of the possibilities that is open to me with regard to my body is to dialogue with it in my journal. That is, in my imagination, to give my body a voice which is different from my own and let it speak out its complaints and groaning. Let me give you an example from the journal of John, who at eighty-four had broken his hip. He wrote this entry when he was in hospital. He had lived a very active life and the fall and the subsequent hospitalization were a considerable setback to him and raised all sorts of questions in his mind.

As in the previous dialogue, when the body speaks the dialogue is written in capital letters.

> Well body you've done it this time. Fancy falling over like that and breaking up. I thought I could trust you. What a mess. I shall be here now for the rest of my life and you will go to pot.
>
> WHO SAYS YOU WILL BE HERE FOR EVER? HIPS CAN HEAL YOU KNOW AND IF YOU HADN'T BEEN SO STUPID YOU WOULDN'T BE HERE AT ALL.
>
> It's no use crying over spilt milk. I fell and you broke. I had relied on you not to do something as stupid as that. I have work to do and I want to get on with it.
>
> HI. STOP A MOMENT. YOU ARE EIGHTY-FOUR AND I AM A BIT OLDER. REMEMBER, OLD CARS DO BREAK DOWN FROM OVER USE OR MISUSE. AS YOU AND I GET OLDER TOGETHER LET'S CONTRACT AND REALIZE THAT WE CAN'T DO THE SAME THINGS WE DID WHEN WE WERE FORTY. THERE IS AN AGEING PROCESS.
>
> Nonsense. I'm as old as I feel and until you put me in here I was perfectly all right. To say that I have to give up now is humbug.
>
> EXACTLY. BUT YOU WILL HAVE TO REALIZE THAT IF YOU WANT TO LIVE AT THE SAME SPEED AS YOU DID BEFORE I BROKE, THEN YOU WILL HAVE TO DO IT WITHOUT ME.
>
> Well if you think I am going to sit down and do nothing you've got another think coming. I am going

to walk and you are going to help me.
OH YES. I WILL HELP. ALL I AM ASKING IS THAT YOU TREAT
ME GENTLY NOW. I AM GETTING OLD.

This conversational dialogue with the body enables the mind of the eighty-four-year-old John to begin looking, not at the fact of the broken hip, but at the whole ageing process. His activity in the past had kept the body fit. His unawareness of getting older made him make the mistake of thinking that what he had accomplished in his youth was still possible today. The body corrects him. Harmony is re-established between his thinking self and the body which supports him. He can now go forward and take it easy without being guilty about it.

When you have a conversation with the body any part of the body may reply. Let its voice be heard. If the elbow wants to speak, let it be heard. If the headache wants to tell you why you have a headache then listen to it. It will stop the headache from recurring if you heed its advice. The same is true of any other part of the body. You write the instruction book for the body as you live it. Learn from the instructions you write. They are part of your historical record; to forget them is to run the risk of reliving them.

My reactions to my body, like the relationships I have with other people are all part of my life history. Their significance is great. They can make or break me. Awareness of their suffering can help me to control the pain I experience within myself. If the symptom has an historical genesis, then write its ladder steps and dialogue with it. Pain within the body, or hurt over a broken relationship, can bring about an equal disability. To carry the pain without dealing with its cause will only add to the disaster. The journal can help you, by making you aware of the true background of the suffering. When it is named and understood there is a possibility of change and healing.

43

5

WHERE AM I GOING?

History is all very interesting but as Mark Twain once said, unless we learn from it then we are doomed to repeat it. That is a very useful warning. Often we find that within the unchartered movement of life, unconsciously we repeat certain action patterns. It might be that you have decided to move house, immediately you take a nose-dive into a deep depression which is very like the depression you had when you last moved house five years ago and ten years before that.

If you look back over the past years then you may well find something in common with all those moves. Perhaps it is the heartbreak of leaving friends, or leaving the home that you have so painstakingly built, or the society of which you have been an important part. The grief process takes time to heal.

History, if it is to be constructive, needs to hand on its lessons in a practical way. If I am going to move house, then before I start the whole planning process it might be good to construct the ladder steps of previous moves. Jane wrote the following:

> Moved from Australia to England.
> Very depressed.
> Eventually got to know people and was very happy.
> Moved from Enfield to Barking.
> Very depressed.
> Got to know people, but didn't feel that there were any deep relationships – it was as though I was

afraid that if I got really close then there would be
another move.
Moved from Barking to Slough.
Depressed and a hospital admission.
The psychiatrist helped me to see that the move from
Australia to England was the cause of my
unhappiness. I relived a lot of the trauma of that
time. Particularly leaving my grandmother whom I
never ever saw again.
Moved from Slough to here in Dorking.
Depressed.
Made friends quickly. Still a little wary though.
Now on the move again this time to Scotland.
Already feel strange and alone – it feels even farther
away from Australia.

Those ladder steps tell us a lot about Jane – the loneliness
experienced as depression; the loss of her home in Australia and
the subsequent death of her grandmother. Moves had become
equated with loss, and although after a time there is a kind of
finding it is done with a wariness that embraces a fear of further
loss.

Jane was able to dialogue in her journal with 'Loss'.

Well here we are again – you and I seem to be
permanent bedfellows. You have your way with me;
you take away all that is significant and leave me with
nothing. I hate you. Life seems so unfair because of
you.
COME OFF IT. YOU ARE DROPPING INTO MY LAP AND
GIVING ME POWER OVER YOU. AND I AM ENJOYING IT.
Get out, you make me sick. You know how
difficult moving is. I shall lose all my friends, my
good neighbours, the handymen who make life
easier.
WELL YOU HAVE ALWAYS FOUND FRIENDS, YOU HAVE
ALWAYS FOUND PEOPLE TO DO THE ODD JOBS THAT NEED
DOING. I AGREE THAT IT IS HARD HAVING TO DO IT ALL

OVER AGAIN, ESPECIALLY WHEN YOU HAVE BEEN HAPPY IN ONE PLACE. BUT LIFE MOVES ON. YOU MOVE ON. LEARN FROM YOUR EXPERIENCE. COUNT THE BLESSINGS OF THE MANY MOVES YOU HAVE HAD TO MAKE BECAUSE OF YOUR JOB . . .

Loss had told Jane to look at the thought, not of the downs in moving but of the subsequent delights. Loss also acknowledged the difficulties of losing friends and handymen and so on. Jane was able to look at a new way of facing the approaching move.

Jane found that the time for action was before she moved. She asked herself what was available in her new proposed area. What clubs, churches and activities were already there with welcoming arms to greet her arrival? She asked lots and lots of questions. Her journal helped her sort out her priorities. Finally she gave a 'thank you' party to her friends and handymen. Many brought her presents for her new life. There were tears of course in parting, but there was also an expectancy for the future. Life is an adventure and for the first time ever she moved without too deep a depression.

When I begin to look forward in my life, my past always comes to the fore. The answers to the future need my record of the past but I must not allow that past to cloud or block the proposed action. To do so would be to give that past a power over me that it does not possess. I have to face the bogeys of the past in order that the future can take shape.

I have always found lists helpful for forward planning. I make a shopping list before I venture into town. I do so, because my past experience tells me that I get very annoyed, if not downright angry and aggressive, when I return without the vital object that I went to buy in the first place. I make lists of things that need to be done. I have even been known to make lists of lists!

Each list has an important purpose. The main reason for the list is to help me remember what it is that needs to be done or bought. If the list is there, then I feel responsible for its fulfilment. I have no one to blame but myself if the list is left unfulfilled. Not to have the list in the first place is to run the risk of forgetting.

From what I said in this chapter so far it is obvious that we are now really beginning to look ahead. Lists can help us to come to terms with the future. They can objectify what it is that needs attention well before the date so that the unexpected doesn't creep up on me and cause that dreaded reaction.

There are two kinds of lists. The first is the shopping list variety, where you sit down and think out exactly what it is that you want to buy. You will put the list into some kind of order. If you are going to the supermarket then it is a good idea to list the items you want to purchase in the order that you expect to find them on the shelves.

The second list could well be called a brainstorming list. This list is written as quickly as possible in order to reduce the risk of judgement or censorship.

Let me give you an example of what I mean.

Eric has been asked to run the village fête. He has never done the job before and he doesn't want the fête to be as awful as the last one. He decided to list the things that came into his mind about the fête.

1. Why must it be during the day?
2. Let's have it at night.
3. Get a bar and a licence to sell drink.
4. Make sure that there is a children's refreshment tent.
5. Lights around the ground.
6. A band display.
7. Some dancing displays.

8. Colour-lighted booths with things for sale.
9. Some form of competition which ends at the fête.
10. Sell tickets for the fête before the date.
11. Tickets to have a lucky number and a prize attached that will only be won if the ticket is produced at the fête.
12. Get the senior school involved.
13. Make it a tattoo sort of thing.
14. Horses?
15. Dog of the Year show with jumps, etc.
16. Hot dogs.
17. Country dancing.
18. Ten-minute intervals between displays to give time to get a drink or visit the stalls.
19. Good display programme.
20. Get each of the pubs to do a display.
21. Procession to the fête field.
22. Make sure it involves the whole family.
23. Publicity needs to be personalized.
24. Make sure that I don't do everything.
25. Instead of a committee have a decision-making body with someone checking that things are done by specific dates. Then let people be adult and get on with their own arrangements within prescribed areas.

I have given you only twenty-five points of Eric's list of over two hundred, to give you an idea of what goes on a list like this.

Eric wrote his list very quickly. The result was interesting. Instead of coming up with the usual time for the fête he has made it into an illuminated tattoo affair with a bar and displays. He has thought about how to get people involved and how to sell admission tickets before the event. He has even thought about the possibility of people buying tickets and then not turning up for the event. Some of these things may not be possible for the village because of the size of the village community. That doesn't matter. They are on the list because Eric wrote quickly, not allowing his brain time to censor the idea.

Lists can be prioritized and revised. Certain things can be deleted from Eric's list when he has time to go through it with someone else. New thoughts can be added and impossible ones deleted. The point of the list has been to get action for the future under way now and to prevent the debacle of last year happening all over again.

A good point to remember when journal writing with lists is that if you think of a point put it down on paper now. Good ideas, like dreams, have a habit of disappearing. The golden rule is, 'Note it now.'

Lists can be made for any number of projects, especially the ones that are personal to you. We shall be using them a lot as we tackle the subject of 'Where am I going?' in this chapter.

Looking towards the future is never easy. If I am honest I would prefer things to go on as they are now until I retire, turn up my toes and quietly pass away. Or would I? Isn't there something else that I would like to do with my life?

Where is my own particular journey taking me? What ambitions do I have for the future? Where do I want to be in ten years' time? With whom do I hope to be sharing my life at that time? How do I want to be spending my time?

It is strange that once one begins to ask these questions all sorts of fantasies begin to form in the mind. Suddenly one becomes aware that the present place is certainly not where I hope to be in the future.

It might be that I hope for a promotion or a move; it might be that it will be time to retire from one job and start something new. It could be that I have become aware that my present partner will no longer be part of my own expected on-going life journey. Or I might feel that I must take some effort to ensure that my relationship with my partner is cherished and renewed in order that we can face the future together.

The fantasy, if it is a possibility and it is really what you want to do, affects the present and the action that needs to be taken in the present 'now' moment. There is therefore a pressing necessity that the plan is fully understood so that its potential can become a reality. It is good to have some idea of the intended destination so that one is at least walking in the right direction now.

Re-read the journal entries that you made when working through Chapter Two of this book; the entries where you examined what was happening in your life at the present moment.

Now, with a sheet of paper in front of you and with your pen at the ready, close your eyes ... relax yourself ... in your silence allow those present events to present themselves to you ... let the film of your life show itself on the screen of your mind's eye ... now let the tenor of the film change ... what will your life be like in ten years' time? ... think and see yourself into the year two thousand and beyond ... what will have changed for you? ... what would you have liked to change? ... who will you be living with or like to be living with? ...

As you do this exercise write down in your journal the answer to the questions. After recording the answers then return to the silence and move on to the next question.

Now comes the most difficult part of the exercise. In the silence consider what must die in your pattern of living in order that the way you see your life evolving in the next ten years may come about ... write down the answers.

In order for the dynamic of life to take place then we have to leave behind people and possessions. If you think that you might be living in Australia or Scotland or any other place in the world, then you have to leave behind friends who have supported you in your present community. You may well have to abandon certain ways of living your life. You might have to leave behind a member of the family who wishes to remain in the present place. If you are emigrating then you might be saying goodbye to elderly relatives whom you might never see again. Write down how you feel about the thought of each and every projected loss. Use the dialogue journal method to express your feelings. At the end of a dialogue session ask yourself the pertinent question, 'What do I want to do with this now?' It may be that you need to express your feelings to your parents before leaving for Australia, bringing into the open the fact that you might never see them again in this life. It is better to face these thoughts rather than to bottle them up. A feeling not expressed can so easily become a depression.

This may well be a painful exercise, but unless you face the unpleasant task before it takes place you might stop the process before it has come to birth. Be forewarned and you will be forearmed. There are unpleasant as well as joyful things ahead.

Another way of tackling future expectations is to list the thousand things you would like to do in the next ten years.

Write the list as quickly as possible; remember, no censorship or judgements. The list may seem completely foolish as you write it, with little or no seeming possibility of any of the ideas ever being accomplished. Put them in the list anyway.

Molly, at seventy-seven years old, wrote that she would like to ice skate in the next ten years! She thought it ridiculous at the time but for her seventy-eighth birthday the journalling group took her to the ice rink and they tried it out. She thoroughly enjoyed herself. Thankfully she didn't fall and hurt herself, due to the group's care in ensuring that two experienced skaters held her between them as they glided gracefully across her once prohibited sphere.

Len at twenty-eight was fed up with his job and in his list

wrote that he would like to go around the world. He spent the next three years planning every detail and then started out to complete the project by actually doing it.

Ideas often come though writing lists, that don't come in any other way. It is sometimes the speed with which a list is written that enables one to dare to write down a dream and then be able to say, 'But why not?'

Finally, for this exercise, ask yourself the following questions:

1. Am I sure that this is the way forward for me?
2. What signs are there that this way is the correct one? Are there alternatives? If so what are they?

Again look at your lists and if necessary revise them to incorporate the new possibilities.

When you have completed this exercise leave it for a month and then come back to it in order to check it out. During the month it will have worked on your unconscious mind and you may well have had a dream or two about it and been able to work with them in the way suggested in Chapter Three of this book. Add to the entry anything that seems relevant to the proposed path. Are there any questions which you need to ask? Any further information you need to know before you can say, 'Yes, this is the way foward for me'?

Leave the answers for another week and then re-read them. Is there anything that needs to be changed? Change it.

Then begin the whole exercise again. This time, however, visualize your life as it will be in five years' time. As you do this, remember that you will have in view the goal you set yourself for the ten-year period. The questions that present themselves will be slightly different. If you know what you want to achieve in ten years' time, or within a ten-year time span, what are the sort of things that will have to be completed in the next five years? Perhaps it will be that you need to learn a new language, get further educational skills, sell a certain property, invest in a new project, or starting building an ark! All these will form ladder steps towards your ten-year goal.

Remember to write in your journal your hopes and fears. Don't forget to record the things that you will have to leave behind during that five-year period. Letting go is very difficult. You may well have to delegate to others things that you have enjoyed doing yourself in order to allow you more time to attain your goal. Don't take them back when the person finds them too difficult to do!

Don't forget to check through your lists or to make new lists for this five-year period. You might find that some of the items on the ten-year list are now transferable to the five-year one. You will be planning the future.

Once you have expressed your hopes and fears for the five-year goal, you are ready to look at the short-term action. What ought you to be doing during the coming year if the five-and ten-year goals are to be reached?

When you begin to concentrate on the coming year then you are ready to make decisions which will affect the day-to-day course of your life. But do you know how you make decisions? Look back to the ladder exercise and from it make a list of all the decisions that have been made in your life. Against each decision state who made that particular decision. Did you make it, did your parents make it, was it forced on you by circumstances beyond your control?

For many of us it is unusual to make an adult decision about the course of our lives until we are well into or beyond the adolescent period of our development. For many even the decisions about jobs are made by default, following in father's or mother's footsteps. 'I am just a housewife like my mother', or 'I became a doctor like my father', are quite common statements.

53

Sometimes a decision is arrived at about our future by the scripting process initiated by some parental person who makes such statements as 'You would make a good nurse,' or 'You would be good in advertising.' The small inner child within us follows the thought that the speaker would be pleased if we followed the implied advice. Sometimes we make decisions upon these scripting remarks without any deep consideration.

If you would like to check this out for yourself in your journal, just try to answer the following questions:

What did your parents or whoever brought you up say about:

1. Education?
2. Religion?
3. Sex?
4. Money?
5. Relationships?
6. Work?
7. Holidays?
8. Foreigners?

The list is endless.

When answering this sort of question in your journal, don't be surprised to discover how the old proverbs have become a part of your unconscious life and have had a hand in your decision making.

Sylvia wrote:

> My parents were very strict about money. I can still hear them saying, 'Take care of the pennies and the pounds will take care of themselves,' or 'Always save for a rainy day.' The trouble was that when it was raining we never spent the money we had so laboriously saved. Another statement that seemed to obsess my parents was that they should have enough

money for their funerals. All their lives they put away two shillings a week for that eventuality, however hard up they were.

I realize now that many of the decisions I make about money are based upon their theories. I am penny-pinching and always trying to save. I will take a bus ride in order to get washing powder a few pence cheaper in the nearby market. I never add the cost of the bus fare to the price of the powder!

It is when we become aware of the extent to which we are still following those sorts of parental decisions that we need to produce some form of behavioural change.

One man wrote the following about his parents' attitude to education and the consequent results:

My parents believed that an education was the entry to great things. When I was a small boy they were impressed with anyone who had been to the university. My father was a self-made man and went regularly to the Workers' Educational Association classes in order, as my mother would say 'to better himself'. Throughout my life when I lived with my parents, reading and writing were more important than playing with my friends. When I dated my first girl friend I was in the sixth form at the local grammar school. My parents went berserk and told me that my education was more important than girls and that I should make sure that I got my degree before I started thinking about getting married. Once you have your degree the world will be your oyster. I believed them. I can hardly believe that myself at this moment but I did. I gave up girl friends. My head was forever in a book. I felt guilty if I even went swimming. I learnt languages. I studied history. I got a first class degree and I became the biggest bore known to girls anywhere in the world. I find it difficult to relate to anyone on a feeling level at all and I move away from superficial conversations or change them into intellectual discussions which bore others. Once I even thought of taking a course at the university on 'Relationships' and then I realized that it would be adding to my store of knowledge but not in fact achieving the thing I long for most, a loving and sustaining personal relationship. In the States you can get a couple of credits towards your Masters degree in relating! I have become very cynical about education but I can now see that I do have to make some alterations in the way I live my life.

Parental scripting can damage your health. It can also help you to make your own decisions. Here is a journal entry by Colin who had been brought up during the depression days of the 1930s:

My father was what I think we would call today a 'workaholic'. I never remember him ever being still. If I stopped and dreamed a bit or asked why we couldn't have a holiday or even questioned why I never saw my father for weeks on end, my mother would come out with the words that he was busy in order to keep us. And anyway, 'it was better to wear out than rust out.' Father died when he was forty-seven. He had worn out faster than most! Ironic. Mother was always afraid that Father or I would be out of work. The spectre of the dole queue haunted her. Her working-class background and her sense of service kept her in the same mould as my father. She worked. Taking in other people's washing; doing housework and looking after me and my five brothers and sisters. She had to be on the go all the time and I think felt guilty when she wasn't doing something. You couldn't read a book in our house – that wasn't work.

When I got married I decided that I was going to spend time with my wife and family. I found it very difficult but I'm glad I persevered. Now I am nearing

retirement age I look back and think what a fool I
would have been if I had followed my parents advice.
I have worked hard but I have also been in charge of
what I have done rather than let it be in charge of me.

Decisions are not easy to make. If in the past they have all
been made for you or have been made as a result of parental
or cultural scripting then you may well find difficulties. The
best way is to give yourself a time limit. 'I have to make this
decision within the next ten days.' Using your journal, list
on the first day all the positive reasons for carrying out a
particular decision. On the second day list all the reasons
against the decision. On the third day list all the questions
you still have which are unanswered about the proposal. Use
the next few days getting the answers to those questions.
Add the answers to the positive or negative list.

When you have arrived at the final listing leave the records
for at least two days. The unconscious mind does various
permutations without causing too much stress during this
period. Come back fresh to your lists and from all the
knowledge in front of you write down your feelings about
how it would be if the project went ahead. Then write down
the feelings you think you might experience if the project
was aborted. The following day make the decision.

Having once made a decision you will either feel free or
so bad that you wonder if it is all worth while. If the latter
happens, perhaps the following journal exercise will help.

1. In the silence be aware of your life at the present
   moment. Jot down the main things that are
   happening.
2. Coming back to the silence, think of how you would
   like your life to be, with the project under discussion
   completed. Again write down the results of your
   thoughts.

57

3. What is stopping you doing what you want to do? What are the blocks? Write them down. By objectifying them they will have less power over you.
4. What can you do about them?

> (a) Dialogue with each block. Give the block a title and a voice. Speak to it: 'You, block, have always stopped me when I want to move.'
>
> Let the block reply: I AM ENTITLED TO MY SECURITY. WHY SHOULD I ALLOW YOU TO DISRUPT ME!
>
> Let the dialogue continue until it reaches a resolution.
>
> (b) If the proposed plan is being thwarted by a guilt feeling, then try to ascertain whether this is a false guilt (i.e. one you think you should have) or is it true and actual (i.e. a guilt that really does belong to you)? Dialogue with the guilt feeling.

Remember that in all dialogues the silence of awareness is necessary. Allow the block the time to come up with the answer – you don't have to think about it. You will be aware when it has spoken to you and that is what needs to be recorded.

Don't neglect blocks at this stage in your decision-making. If you do, eventually they will come back at you and hit you when you are least expecting them. They could remain with you during the whole new project and spoil it!

Once you have dealt with the immediate blocks you can begin to make the change. Expect the project to succeed. If you don't, there would be no point in making the effort for the change and one of the blocks would have won. Write down in your journal the ladder steps of the change. What exactly has to be done? Write the thoughts down as they come to you; they can be sorted into priorities at a later time. Try not to be overwhelmed at this time with the amount of things that have to be completed. The object of the exercise is to see how many things are going to have to change.

When the list has been completed then rewrite it in order of priorities. In this way you will arrive at the first step. Give that step a completion date. Put that date in your diary. Let the action planned get under way now. Enrol for your language class and make sure you attend (we are all very good at finding excuses not to do something, even when we have decided after much hard work that this is what we really want to do). You are in charge of your life. Enjoy it.

6

LOOKING ROUND

The materialism of the 1980s gave rise to a consumer boom which filled our homes with an increasing number of possessions. A century earlier, a farm labourer would have been able to move house using only one horse and cart. What has happened in the intervening hundred years to our sense of what is necessary to survive?

How do you view your possessions? Are they a pleasure to own and collect, are they necessities or just sheer luxuries? What meaning do they have for you? Would you, if you were cast away on the proverbial desert island, be able to exist without them?

Recently a nun, working in a home for travellers found an old man with bare feet who seemed to be without a pair socks. Being full of good will, she told him that she would give him a pair of socks. He replied that he had a pair of socks but they were being washed. When she said she would find him another pair, he replied, 'But I already have one pair of socks, what would I do with another pair?' It is true that you can only wear one pair of socks at a time, or watch one television, or drive one car.

Materialism, possessiveness, are part of the new divisions which separate society: north versus south, rich versus poor. Justice requires that each person fulfil their potential. It also requires that one part of society does not exploit another to their detriment.

On our own we cannot change society. We can only

change ourselves. Our relationship with our possessions determines much of how others live. The slogan 'Live simply, that others may simply live' needs to be taken seriously.

All this poses a dilema which we have to face. Stated simply it is this — Do I live for myself or do I live for others?

In your journal try to answer that question. I give two examples to show you how others are thinking and to stimulate you in your own thoughts. One comes from Alice, an elderly lady who has enjoyed the comforts of a very long life, another from Larry, a young man who is just setting out on the pilgrimage.

I have just left my childhood home. I have lived in it all my life and the difficulties in turning it out have made me feel very tired, even of life itself. Seventy years in one place makes one very complacent. Things happened and accumulated almost as though I had been unaware. All the memories have been uncovered in the attics now. The old gas lamp mantles, the cases and the hat boxes, the water jugs and basins. All had given way to something new and I realize now that we hoarded what we did not want because we didn't know what to do with it. I feel slightly guilty now, because there are so many people in need. I have come to an old people's home to end my days. I have just one room (my home had twenty-three); a bed, a table and two chairs. There is a basin and hot and cold water. I have a nice fireplace and I can put all the family photographs on the mantelpiece. Many of my meals are brought to me but I can go to the dining room and there is a nice lounge downstairs with a television. It is so much nicer to share with others and I don't feel so lonely as I thought I would. This is all a new experience for me. I feel I have discarded a lot of the clutter of my life. Perhaps now I can think about the deeper things. My journey is not over yet. I had to leave my home, because I couldn't look after it. I thought that would be the end of me but somehow I feel now that I am making a new beginning. All the things I have been taught in the past, all the security I thought I had which would last for ever, seems to be rather useless now. I am, like a nun, in a cell, it is my space and it is big enough. I have a small pension, but it is large enough to supply my needs. I have a renewed faith in a creator who provides for the lilies of the field and although I don't claim to be such a lily, I am provided for and I am thankful. One day I shall have to let go of this life. I cannot take with me all that I am using even at this moment. I am glad that I have turned out of my home (still thankful for the time I had in it) and I am pleased that others will live there. In fact the house is coming down and fourteen others will be built on the site. I can see now how I could have shared all those years ago. I am sorry for that but I am glad that I have done it before it is too late.

I am twenty-three and the greater part of my life has been spent in Thatcher's materialistic Britain. All my thinking has certainly been affected by the 'Get as much as you can' theory of this conservatism. When I at last left home and took a room of my own, my parents, who had been brought up in the Macmillan era of 'You've never had it so good' began to pile up the things I would need. A television set and a video recorder, my stereo system, my walkman, a refrigerator and a washing machine besides the cooker. When I measured them all they wouldn't go in the room – that's a lie, they would go in the room but there wouldn't be enough room for a bed and as far as I could see there wouldn't be room for me either. It was obvious that I had to choose. At that time I walked around the American Museum in Bath and was quite shaken when I saw the simple arrangement of Shaker furniture. Each piece could be suspended from hooks on the walls. Each masterpiece was functional and needed. It really

62

made me think about my own position. I began to look at my needs as opposed to what my parents thought I wanted. I became aware that I was a privileged person in the world and although I can accept that, I also realized that so was everyone else. Independence sounds all right but it doesn't do much for others. Interdependence was what my life was really about. I painted my room white – it reflects a hope and a light. I have a mattress on the floor which doubles as a bed and a sofa. With a large cushion it is very comfortable. I have my walkman but I share the tapes with my friends – we have a sort of library. When we add a new tape we give one of the old ones away. It isn't that I am trying to be good or that I am throwing away the things my parents have given and taught me. Somehow I really don't want to get into the muddle of possessing so much that it stops me from facing the realities of the world in which I have to live out my life. The Shaker masterpieces at the Bath museum made me aware that simplicity is possible with beauty. Lifestyle has become important to me. I never realized the waste when I lived at home. All those dustbins full of irreplaceable world resources. Besides my job, I now have a new life philosophy; it is 'Share what I can, recycle what I can and possess only what I need.'

Both of these entries are looking at a deeper side of life. Possessions are not bad in themselves, it is the way you use them that changes things.

Possessions are not the only things that you need to look at as you pursue the inner pilgrimage. In personal growth terms, we seem only to look at ourselves because in reality it is only ourself that we can change. There is a whole word beyond myself, a world I need to relate to and become involved with.

How do you react to the world in which you live? Do you

have a pessimistic view of society, political parties and trade unions? Or do you think that all is right with the world and the way it is being governed? What is your place in the ongoing life of the area in which you live? How do you make your views known so that things can be changed? Have you made a pen friend of your MP? What is your contribution to the crises of third world countries? Do you help or hinder?

The questions could go on and there are many which you will able to add to the list. The point is that through the journal you can question your role in society and you can change that role. By changing your role you begin the transformation of the world. Bottle banks, national litter days, anti-smoking campaigns all began with someone asking a question and trying to look for an answer.

This leads us to look at the spiritual dimension of life. As you have written your journal you will have noticed how large a part silence plays. In the silence you are joined to the whole collective unconscious. In contemplation there is no subject or object, only a unity. You became one with all that is. You see things not as creator and created but as both. Dualism ceases. Spirituality is the unity of all that is, and in that unity you are both part and whole.

Whatever your religious belief – Christian, Muslim or Hindu – the inner silence of unity is the same. To reach into that silence and to feel the oneness of all that is, would be to enter the realm of heaven. The reaching, and the silence, and the oneness are not objects but part of the whole which is me.

From this inner perspective the world takes on a different aspect. You see with an inner eye and hear with an inner ear the destruction of the rain forests or the harm done by the pollution of the sea. The inner eye and the inner ear, all part of the true self, are part of the destruction and harm. The falling away of dualism allows the true self, created in the beginning, before a fall, to be revealed. You see your face (as a Zen Buddhist would say) before you had a face.

Entering this position, and it is extremely difficult to write about it because one immediately objectifies the very thing that is not object (such is the limited language available), we are caught up into the divine dimension. Whatever we feel, or whatever our parental messages have been, about the creator or saviour, we become one with that which was before us and also with that which will come after us. Our awareness and our availability to this oneness begins to reveal to us the answer to the questions of the universe and our place in that universe.

In our journal exercises, the writing will become shorter and the silences longer as we enter this other area of life. We will become aware that our true self does not know the answer to the world's problems; it is at one with them. We shall be able to hear and be at one with the symphony of creation; we shall weep and jump for joy as each area is brought to our notice. Then, like Julian of Norwich*, we shall be able to say that 'all will be well and all manner of things will be well.'

It is this mystical approach which will bring about both an inner and outer harmony. The true self will be revealed, vulnerable and ready for death, but living because one lives in all that is.

Exercise: What was your face like before you were conceived?

Christine, at seventy-four wrote:

> To see myself before my parents came together is to realize my existence from the beginning of time

*An English mystic who lived in Norwich during the fourteenth century.

– I am one with the face of God; I am one with the world; I am one with the galaxies; I am. I feel, having written like this for the first time in my long life, that at long last I can see the purpose of it all. It is a unity, I am part of it. Whatever I do affects the other parts. We are all one together. We destroy and we build up. I cannot do it alone but I must continue until the end to be part of the creative action. If I fail, then something, somewhere remains undone for a time. The task seems to be great; the vessel seems to be weak; but when I realize that everyone who lives is also part of the working, creating world then I realize for the first time, that in unity with others lies my strength. I am not alone. My prayer can only be, that I shall not fail in the great game which I have called my life. For my failure would affect others. 'I press on towards the goal to win the prize for which God has called me heavenward' (Philippians 3:14)

Derek, at twenty, wrote:

Life is strange. I come from my parents, who in turn come from their parents and so on back and back as far as you can get. Each parent carried within themselves the seed that would one day be me. That is a miracle in itself. In the beginning was my Genesis. I am part of the creation when God creates man and woman in the divine image. I am part of the thought in the mind of a creator God (God only needs to speak and the thought becomes word and action). I live because I am a part of God and God is within me. My face before I was conceived is the image and likeness of God and somehow I like to believe that for a moment in time I was seen in that likeness. I want to return to it; it is what I have been looking for; in it lies my strength, without it I can do nothing, I am false and consequently I do things which bolster up my falseness. To have discovered even for a few minutes this other truer self is to be content.

To have written a paragraph like this will make us look again at the other areas of the journal, particularly those which deal with lifestyle. We shall have to ask ourselves questions like these:

1. How does this affect the way I live?
2. What alterations need to be made in my life pattern?
3. What reconciliations have to be effected in order that I can become one with the world in which I live?
4. What reconciliation am I still seeking from others in order to enter into that inner peace which is to do with the whole rather than the part which is me?

Peter wrote:

> To experience, as I did for a brief moment in the silence, the idea of myself made in the image of God, mirroring the creator, is awesome. I believe that the idea is a truth which I have never before considered. How am I to deal with it in my life? If I mirror the face of a creator, then in what way am I a part of that creating act? Certainly not by the way I live out my life? Creating is a joyful occupation and yet I spend my time destroying trees in the rain forests in order to make land available for agriculture. I have, until this moment in time, always considered this to be a worthwhile thing to be doing. It helps others. Scientifically I know it will all become a dust bowl in a matter of years. My answer has always been that perhaps it will – but for the moment it is helping someone who needs land in order to grow food, in order to live. Now I am not sure. The whole ecological system is so interdependent; the rain forests are needed, they are part of the creator's (my) work. Can I go on destroying them? The answer is a definite 'No'. I must change my job.

Peter did change his job. He is working for the conservation council now. His journal experience brought him face-to-face with himself. He could change. He chose to change and went through with it. We are faced with certain dilemmas in the same way. To change them requires courage and determination and perhaps a different lifestyle. Are we up to the challenge?

The personal journal is a book which records your growth as a human being. It is a tool of self-knowledge. In this way it records your own history and puts that history in the context of the cosmic dimension. Spiritual history is also important. It records our beginnings (the whole creative act). It spells out the inner journey with its successes and its failures (in much the same way that the Bible records the journeys of the Hebrew Israelites) and its looks forward to the future.

Andrew, a theological student wrote:

> Until Brian suggested it to me I had never thought of the Bible as the story of my life and I want to see if that is true by writing in this journal.
>
> I believe that death, judgement, heaven and hell are part of my present and on-going life.
>
> I went through a long period in my early twenties when everything was sheer blackness; I was jilted by the girl friend of my schooldays — I lost a very good job where I was making a lot of money and seemed all set on a golden career in the city. Both of my parents were killed in a car crash and this meant selling up our family home. I found myself looking back, and like Lot's wife (Genesis 19:26), I became very bitter. I also felt very trapped. I suppose I had come to the land of exile but I didn't know at the time who or what I was exiled from.
>
> Then came that experience of the burning bush (Exodus 3:2) or my own personal Damascus Road (Acts 9:3). I was sitting in great gloom in a cellar bar. I can think of it now as my lion's den (Daniel 6:16). My friends had just left and I thought I wanted

another drink. I went to the bar to get a beer but was handed a glass of red wine. I took it and found myself pulled into a small party of people who were celebrating a birthday. I drank the toast and distinctly heard someone say, 'It is like a communion.' I didn't wait around or question the meaning of those words. But they wouldn't go away. I was in exile from myself and from all that had meaning. I wanted communion with my fellows; I wanted communion with a girl and then, suddenly, I knew that I wanted communion with someone other – God, Jesus, Buddha or whoever. Someone that was greater than all the mess that I seemed to be in. I know what Paul's blindness must have felt like; or for that matter the descent of Christ into the hell of the dark grave. I was desperate and didn't know where to go. Eventually I found myself in a quiet church and I sat and stared at a painting of the Last Supper. I realized that in the communion there was great joy, there was service (Jesus washed the disciples' feet) but there was also an awareness of the agony to come. They went out and it was night – blackness – despair – depression. They were all part of my own feelings. I found a Bible and read and re-read the story of the passion and death of the Son of God. It all seemed so pointless and evil, death had finally triumphed over goodness and light. I felt almost suicidal. I also didn't know what to do. It was at my lowest point that the miracle happened – I suddenly became aware that I was not alone in the church. From a far vestry came the voices of a choir singing 'I am the resurrection and I am the life.' I began putting together the words, communion, service, joy, feeding, bread, wine, agony and death but now I added the words resurrection and new life. Was it really a possibility for me? I realized that I had last heard the words 'I am the resurrection' when my parents' bodies had been taken into the crematorium. I had thought them insulting at the time and without possible belief. Now I was stunned – had I gone through my own death and was I now awaiting my resurrection, my new life, and if so, what was it to be?

As I have come to know the Bible better I am aware now of how many parallels there are between what happened to a people and what has happened to me. There has been a transfiguration. I am no longer what I appeared to be. I have died to the old bitterness and saltiness; I have a vision of myself coming up out of my own Egypt of death and slavery; I am, from those far-off days anyway, a resurrected person who is trying to lead a different kind of life. I have a model now, who went about living his life to the full; becoming what he truly was and is, the Son of God. My full potential will be to follow in his footsteps – to serve – to rejoice – to feed others with the energy that is in bread and wine – to face the agony and the pain within myself and others – to rise again and again in order that the new life which is Christ may be apparent in me.

Andrew went on to become a priest. He serves in an East End parish where the agony and the ecstacy are apparent. Somehow he gets alongside people because he recognizes in himself the wounded healer.

There is an old saying that when God made us he gave us two ears and only one mouth. Perhaps we are meant to listen twice as long before we speak. Listening to the inner voice, pondering and meditating upon what we hear – writing it and discussing it in our journal – will, I believe, bring us to a deeper understanding not only of ourselves but of God.

Materialism, possessions, spirituality have all been discussed in this chapter. I hope that the thoughts have been useful to you and will help you in writing your own spiritual history. Use the ladder steps to get you started.

70

Use dialogues to get you out of the traps that will surround you. Use dialogues to speak in meditation to the principal characters of the story. Use lists to tease out the unspoken thoughts about your way of life. Above all, become aware in order that you can live wholly.

7

THE REVIEW

When you have written an entry in your journal, what do you do with it? The journal is a work book. It is not something that will lie around unread, stuffed into the bottom of a drawer. It contains the substance of which your life is made. It is a book that will inspire you, frustrate you, and impinge in a number of ways on the direction your life is taking. It will tell of the ways in which you make decisions. It records the mobility of life and how it relates to your place in the cosmos. If it is anything other than this, your journal will be just another historical diary that will collect dust.

There is a need to review what you have written over a given period — perhaps every three months, or annually. Re-read the pages of your journal. Pick out the entries that still have not come to any meaningful resolution or changed your pattern of behaviour. Jot down under today's date what energy there remains in those entries. You might come to the conclusion that what you had hoped for three months ago is now no longer necessary or desirable. If so, make a note to that effect and bring the entry to a satisfactory completion. It is releasing some of the ideas or supposed needs of the past, or even some traditions, that enables us to move towards the next hurdle.

Periodic reviews are necessary in job evaluations, in marriages and in other spheres of daily living. Looking back helps us to learn from our history and minimizes the extent to which we shall repeat it. Repetition is a recycling of life rather than a creative forward drive. It is usually unnecessary, and is often a waste of time. Time is precious and we need to squeeze from it as much as possible if we are to fulfil our potential.

Reviews help us to look realistically at what has been accomplished in the past year, decade or even half-century. They also help us to look forward to the future. Shopkeepers take stock for several reasons.

1. To assess what particular line has been a best-seller.
2. To assess what line has been a failure, or is no longer necessary to the enterprise at this time.
3. To look expectantly at the new products and to ascertain how they can best be displayed and sold.
4. To assess the annual turnover and to see how it can be increased.

In taking stock of our lives the same procedure is necessary. In marriage for instance we can ask:

1. What has been particularly good about this marriage? What are the things we have enjoyed about it and want to keep? How can those things be enjoyed more often?
2. What are the things that have been good but are now no longer a necessary part of the marriage – the things that may well have taken a lot of time but are no longer necessary in that form? What has to be released in this marriage in order that other things can come into existence?
3. What are the new aspects of the marriage that need to be worked with in order to keep it dynamic and growth-fulfilling?
4. How can we make better what we already have?

By writing down the answers to some of these questions people have found out that they are holding on to things that are no longer relevant to the particular stage of growth; that energy is expended where it is not necessary, leaving little for the new and creative aspect of the ongoing relationship.

With a sheet of paper in front of you, date it, and then write down the answer to the question, 'How do I feel about my marriage at the present moment?' When you have completed the exercise read the following journal entry. Phyllis had just celebrated her ruby wedding anniversary.

The celebration party went well. Everyone enjoyed it and Bill and I were kept busy ensuring that our usual and expected standard of hospitality was as high as ever.

The party has given me time to look back and review forty years of marriage and at the same time to realize that, because we were married when I was just eighteen, it is possible that we could have thirty or forty more years together. Wow! Somehow that was a shock. It is not that the marriage has been bad. I suppose it has been like the curate's egg, good in parts and hell in other places. The thought that it could go on for another forty years has brought me up with a jolt. I don't want to get out of it but I don't want it to be the same either – that would be just boring and, I feel, not very productive.

The first years were spent bringing up the children and I thoroughly enjoyed that. I am enjoying looking after the grandchildren as well and expecting a great-grandchild soon. My role of mother goes on and on.

Bill has the business and that is his baby; it still is. The problems are the same – always teaching someone new to work this machine or to do that job. His role as 'The Boss' goes on and on too.

When I look back at my own parents' marriage it was much the same. You could tell the time of day by watching them. Dad would always arrive for lunch at five past one and leave again at five to two. You could tell the day of the week by what was for

74

lunch – roast on Sunday, cold meat on Monday, cottage pie on Tuesday, and so on. It never changed throughout their married life. They were as solid as the rock of Gibraltar. There were highlights like Christmas and Easter and birthdays but otherwise it was the same old routine, year in year out. They were happy in their way but after Dad's retirement they just faded away and were both dead within the year. I never expected much from them and I suppose they never expected much from me. They were a case of recycling if ever I saw one. They established a way of life in their first year of marriage and they repeated it until they died. It was a good formula for them. I know I don't want to repeat it but deep down I feel that I might.

I have learnt since starting on this journal that I have to look at the good things of my marriage but I also need to look at what really can be freed at the present moment. This is the hard bit; I don't want to be a possessive mother but I know I am. Donald, my eldest boy, said the other day that he always dressed in his short trousers when he came to see me. He was joking of course – or was he? Margaret, our next door neighbour, only sees her children once or twice a year. She says that they are all good friends and while she has her health they are all capable of looking after themselves as grown up adults. Perhaps if I am to enjoy this next stage of my marriage I need to make friends out of my children rather than worrying all the time about whether they have done their washing! Does it really matter to me if they haven't, and why do I get so uptight about it all anyway? Am I repeating my parents' pattern? Recycling their lives? God forbid. But when I think about it like this I sometimes feel it is true. When I was thirty, mother still asked me if I had clean underwear on when I went out. I laughed at the time, thinking that she still considered me a child of five. But perhaps that is the way I still look at my family and I need to stop it – let go of that thought – allow them to become adults and get on with their own lives.

Bill needs to put in a manager and allow the business to grow up as well. We'd have some time together then to do some of things we have always talked about but never had the energy to carry out. We could even get more involved in outside things. The potential is enormous ... but could we really change?

Just re-reading what I have written I realize how little I am involved. I have written about the children and the grandchildren and the expected great-grandchild and about Bill and the business. But what about the real me? Do I really exist as a person in my own right or am I just some other person's need?

Reflective writing like this enables the individual to look at, review and then suggest possible ways in which change can be made. It is only by reviewing the past that we see what has actually happened in life rather than what we think happened. Sometimes, as Phyllis realized, the past is being recycled by the following generation. If that is true in your life, be warned; we are inclined to recycle the mistakes and the disasters as well as the better points of history.

The image of this marriage was a roundabout. The horses were going up and down, but sedately. There was nothing extraordinary about it at all.

When Phyllis repeated the exercise a week later, the image had changed, and like the scene in the Mary Poppins film, each of the horses rode away from the roundabout into the fields and away to adventure.

When writing about this second image, Phyllis was able to say that she and her husband had talked about the staleness of their marriage relationship and they had made plans to change it.

If you find that you are like Phyllis and want to change,

then very quickly write a list of things you would really like to do. Try to write it quickly so that your inner censor won't erase from your mind all the things you feel you would like to do. Don't be afraid of this brainstorming technique. Once the list is written it can be revised and you may well be able to ask, 'Well, so why not?'

It can be a good idea to write a marriage review at the time of your wedding anniversary. Looking back over the year will highlight the growth in the relationship. It is also a good time to look forward to the coming year, and if the review can be done with both parties then it helps if you each write a series of lists:

Bill writes three lists:

1. What I would like for Bill during this coming year.
2. What I would like for Phyllis during this coming year.
3. What I would like for our marriage during this coming year.

Phyllis writes three lists:

1. What I would like for Phyllis during this coming year.
2. What I would like for Bill during this coming year.
3. What I would like for our marriage during this coming year.

When you have both completed the lists, bring them together, and where the 'likes' are the same determine to do something about them. For example, Bill has written, 'I would like to visit India but it means leaving Phyllis.' Phyllis has written, 'I would like Bill to be able to visit India.' The opportunity to talk this through with each other has now presented itself. Phyllis is eventually able to say that she would like to be away for a part of the year and wants to be on her own. Bill goes to India. Phyllis has space for her own thing. Neither has impeded the other; there is no space for resentments to arise because it has been talked about in an adult manner and a decision reached.

The important points for growth will be found in the lists, provided that each party is being perfectly honest about their hopes. Bill and Phyllis' images were centred around the theatre, which they both enjoyed. Phyllis saw the future as the start of the third act, when everything would be resolved. Bill saw a new production at a new theatre!

The New Year is a good time to write a review of what has happened in the past year and what expectations there are for the future. It is also a good time to re-read your journal entries from the previous year.

The periodic work review can also be handled through a journal entry.

Delia wrote:

> I hate review time, but I always feel better when I have done it. The past year has been a disaster, family-wise. Mother and Father died within five months of each other. They have left a really big hole in my life and I don't think I am coping with it very well. I feel lonely and there is always something I want to tell them and then realize that they are not there.
>
> Work has been chaotic. Marian, my boss, set certain specific targets for me at the beginning of the year. I had to complete a survey of the sales force; decide how many more sales people were required and find them. To rewrite the sales promotion literature and to update the training conferences for the new intakes. To retrain all the old representatives.
>
> It didn't seem a lot. The hassle has been terrible. I have felt like giving the job up several times and the illness of my parents and their deaths didn't help. I

don't want to make them an excuse but I must admit
that I felt particularly under the weather trying to
cope with everything.

I enjoyed re-writing the sales promotion literature
and taking the training conferences for the new
intake. The updating of the old crowd was much
more difficult and I know that I didn't do it very well
. . .

Delia's image is of a blank wall, that is covered in black
paint.

In her journal entry the main points of life are highlighted.
The death of relatives influences work procedures however
much we would like to say it makes no difference. There is
a need to be able to write about her parents, to objectify the
grief process and hopefully come to terms with it. Delia was
able to look back at the horrors and the successes of the year.
She admits the failure with the older sales group and is then
able to look forward to the new year and her superior's
expectations and forward plans. Perhaps she needs to record
her feelings about failure with the sales group. How does
she, a competent executive, feel about this failure on her
part? What lessons has she learnt from it? How can such a
situation be avoided in the future?

Delia's blank wall image, with its dark black paint, mirrors
the inner feeling of loneliness and despair. It is a grief
reaction to her parents' death, but it is also triggered by her
own feeling of failure in her job. Job evaluations and reviews
need, like confessions, to start with thanksgiving for the
good things that have been achieved. It is much easier to face
the failures then.

The review procedure will be helped if you have kept a
good daily journal. Most of the work will already have been
done and you only have to bring it together to write the
actual evaluation.

Please, please, find time to write this daily journal. It need take only ten minutes at the end of the day but the information it contains will be of inestimable value in the years ahead. I have found that whenever I become depressed or face a grief reaction, it is time to look back at previous times when this has happened. If I have faithfully recorded the progress of the depression or the grief then I will have noted the upward swing – the pathway out of the darkness. I will also have written down the actual springboard event. It might have been a good meal with a friend, a long hot bath or a good raging cry. Whatever it was, it served as a trigger mechanism to help me come to terms with the blackness. It oftens works a second time. The long road to recovery becomes shorter the second time round, especially when I know the way out because I have already recorded it.

8

GOING ON FROM HERE

Personal growth is about being in charge of one's own life. Much of our time is already mortgaged to others – our employers, our families, our outside interests and work for the good of the community. Hopefully much of that time is being spent in doing things we enjoy. In my journal counselling practice I am aware of an inner unhappiness which results from work that is not fulfilling and is being performed in a desultory way until such time as the pension comes around.

Growth needs personal satisfaction. Without it, I become moribund. This satisfaction comes from all levels of life – from my work, my family, my hobbies, my spirituality. If there is a dissatisfaction in any of these areas the others will be affected or they will be over-stressed. The following extract comes from the journal of Lillian:

> There is within me a deep disturbance. I cannot rightly name it, but nothing seems really worthwhile.
>
> My work at the shirt factory passes seven hours of every day from Monday to Friday. My work-mates are noisy and full of superficial fun. I join in, because it is something to do. Sometimes I feel I, and they, go a little too far and that there is a sort of malicious spite in what we are saying and thinking about other people.
>
> When I get home at night, after I have done the shopping, I prepare the same old meals and watch the same old ghastly soap operas on television before going to bed. I feel too tired to go out.
>
> I resent the children their freedom and the way

they live their lives with their partners.

I am aware that there is very little satisfaction from my church. Once everything was fine. I believed in God. I could sing rousing choruses. But that has all gone. I feel as though there is no point in that any more.

Time is beginning to hang heavily. I know that I must adjust to being a widow. I know that my life hasn't ended (although at times I wish it had). I know that I am the only person who can do anything about it. But I don't know how and no one seems able to help me. Writing it all down has at least got the bile and seemingly hurtful things outside myself and I have wanted that for a long time.

From my writing I can see that:

I am still grieving my husband. I need help. I thought I could do it on my own; that I would get over his death (it's nearly two years now) but I haven't. I wonder if CRUSE can help?

I need to look at the job. I'm not really happy there any longer. Perhaps I need something that will bring me into contact with a different sort of people – I don't know. I mustn't lose sight of this. I need to be more attentive to the family without intruding into their lives. A little more energy would make me a better grandmother.

I need outside stimulation. I don't know where to go for this but I resolve to start looking around.

Through journal writing this lady has been able to name the areas of her unhappiness. To name a sorrowful area allows you to take command of it, rather than allowing it to destroy you. In her journal she can now ask herself these questions

1. What can I do for myself in this situation?
2. Who can I ask for help?
3. Can I accept the things that cannot be changed?

The lady is able to answer the first two quite easily and already she has decided to ask CRUSE (the counselling organization for the bereaved) for help. The third question is not so easy to answer.

If I allow the things that cannot be changed to continue to control my life then I am using energy in a fruitless way. In the example, Lillian cannot bring back her husband. Acceptance is a part of the grieving process and it is hoped that the counsellors she suggests contacting will help her to come to an acceptance of her husband's death. Until this happens she will continue to think and act as a helpless, unwanted person. Her thoughts will be concerned with the bargaining areas of bereavement: 'If only I had him back then I would ...' This would be a misplaced use of her energy and would serve only to deepen the sense of disturbance. Recording the death in the journal (and note that she does not mention her husband's name) as a simple statement of fact, would help her in the growth process. 'Bill died on the 5th June 19 ... I am devastated. I know I can never bring him back.'

To record the fact is not necessarily to accept it. It is a way of beginning the process of inner acceptance. When re-reading the journal that particular sentence will eventually have the psychological effect of bringing about the reality and finality of Bill's death. Time and the journal work together.

The diary organizes time. The journal reviews time. My actions today, according to my diary timetable, are reviewed against a background of personal history. They are thus put into the context which goes to make up the unique me. Others will have been through the same experiences but their journal entries will be completely different. Two people watching a royal wedding will give entirely diverse accounts of the event. The same would be true of witnesses to a crime. The timings (the diary event) would be the same, all else, because of the subjective viewpoint, will alter. It is sometimes said that it is hard to realize that two people have been at the same meeting, so different are their accounts of what actually took place.

Time, in journal terms, is about purpose and the tasks needed to fulfil that purpose. The down-to-earth action becomes a diary entry in order that the overall purpose can be fulfilled. The nitty-gritty of daily living is only of significance in the way it impinges upon the overall life purpose.

Purpose is about meaning and direction. Without it we drift, and consequently say at the end of a tiring day, 'I have worked hard all day but accomplished nothing.' The truth is that I have accomplished nothing which has furthered my purpose, and inwardly I sense that the things I have done are worthless. Inwardly this is unsatisfactory and can give rise to resentment and bitterness.

If it is possible, share your journal entries with a counsellor, friend or spouse. Read the entries to them, particularly the entries which disturb you. Listen to their comments. If they seem relevant (they won't always be relevant) and question the writing, note down the areas that need to be reviewed in light of their comments. Ask yourself how you can deal with these areas in your journal. Do I need to tease out that dream sequence a little more? Was it telling me something that I have missed? Do I need to dialogue with my work (giving my work a voice) in order to get in touch with what I am really doing? Would it be a good time to review what really happened at the time of my divorce? How is my past imprisoning my present enjoyment of life? What is the next step for me?

Journal writing is fun. Write a poem about that beautiful moment when you first saw your lover. Paint a picture of the sunset. Write across the page, around the page, from the middle of the page. Express yourself. Let the real you explode on the page. Be in charge of your life. Your life, like your pen, is in your hands.

BIBLIOGRAPHY

Adams, Kathleen, *Journal to the Self*, Warner Books 1990

Augustine, St, *Confessions*, Everyman Library 1907

Benn, Anthony Wedgwood, *Out of the Wilderness. Diaries 1963–67*, Hutchinson 1987

Broyles, Anne, *Journalling*, The Upper Room, Nashville 1988

Cargas, H. and Radley, R., *Keeping a Spiritual Journal*, Nazareth Books (Doubleday) 1981

Colville, John, *The Fringes of Power. Downing Street Diaries 1939–1955*, Hodder and Stoughton 1985

Doubtfire, Dianne, *Teach Yourself Creative Writing*, Teach Yourself Books (Hodder) 1983

Fox, George, *Journal*, Cambridge University Press

Frank, Anne, *The Diary*, Pan Books 1989

Hammarskjöld, Dag, *Markings*, Faber 1964

Hawker, Brian, *Spiritual Pathways*, Marshall Pickering

Hawker, James, *A Victorian Poacher*, Oxford University Press 1961

Holden, Edith, *The Country Diary of an Edwardian Lady*, Webb and Bower 1977

Kelsey, Morton T., *Adventure Inward*, Augsburg Publishing House 1980

Kilvert, Francis, *Kilvert's Diary*, Ed. W. Plomer, Penguin 1977

Macmillan, Harold, *Riding the Storm*, Macmillan 1971

——*Pointing the Way 1959–61*, Macmillan, 1972

Merton, Thomas, *The Sign of Jonas*, Hollis Carter

Osborn, Lawrence, *Dear Diary*, Grove Books Ltd

——*Paper Pilgrimage*, Darton, Longman and Todd 1990

Progoff, Ira, *At a Journal Workshop*, Dialogue House, New York 1982

——*The Practice of Process Meditation*, Dialogue House, New York 1982

——*The Symbolic and the Real*, Conventure, London

Rainer, Tristine, *The New Diary*, Angus and Robertson 1980

Simons, George, *Keeping your Personal Journal*, Paulist Press 1987

Bibliography

Wales, Gerald of (Giraldus Cambrensis), *The Journey through Wales*, Penguin Classic

Woolman, John, *The Journal of John Woolman*, Everyman Library

Details of Journal Writing Courses can be obtained from:

The Conference Secretary,
Emmaus House,
Clifton Hill,
Bristol BS8 4PD

The Conference Secretary,
Post Green House,
Lytchett Minster,
Poole,
Dorset BH16 6AP

The Conference Secretary,
Radford Hall,
Southam Road,
Radford Semele,
Leamington Spa,
Warwickshire CV31 1FH.